3-53

DECREE ON
PRIESTLY TRAINING

AND

DECREE ON
THE MINISTRY AND
LIFE OF PRIESTS

DECREE ON
PRIESTLY TRAINING
OF
VATICAN COUNCIL II

and

DECREE ON
THE MINISTRY AND
LIFE OF PRIESTS
OF
VATICAN COUNCIL II

Commentary by
Frank B. Norris, S.S.

1966
VATICAN II DOCUMENTS

PAULIST PRESS
(Paulist Fathers)
Glen Rock, New Jersey

Nihil Obstat:
Rev. James J. O'Connor
Censor Librorum

Imprimatur:
✠ Leo A. Pursley, D.D.
Bishop of Fort Wayne-South Bend
August 27, 1966

Library of Congress
Catalog Card Number: 66-29072

Cover Design: Claude Ponsot

Published by the Paulist Press
Editorial Office: 304 W. 58th St., N.Y., N.Y. 10019
Business Office: Glen Rock, New Jersey 07452

Printed in the
United States of America
by Our Sunday Visitor Press

CONTENTS

7

Decree on Priestly Training

Commentary

Introduction

"Now the moment has arrived for a searching examination. Vatican Council II must create a new kind of seminary in line with the needs of today. If there is one place where Pope John's *aggiornamento* is needed, it is here." So spoke Cardinal Léon Suenens of Malines-Brussels at a Rome press conference in October, 1964, during the third session of the Council. These words expressed his personal concern of many years' standing, as well as that of large numbers of his fellow bishops. It was their deep conviction that the updating of seminaries is not just another desired result of Vatican Council II. In considerable measure the ultimate success or failure of the Council will depend upon the sort of priests that seminaries will prepare for ordination during the next two or three generations. The Latin adage states: "Talis grex qualis rex"—as the leader, so the flock. If the priestly ministers of the Christian community are equal to the challenge of the Council, the likelihood of an effective renewal of

13

the Church at the grass-roots level is strong. Otherwise, it is slight indeed.

But why "a new kind of seminary"? Because we are, even now, living in a "new Church". The seminary brought into being by the Council of Trent (1545-1563) faithfully reflected the 16th-century Church's understanding of itself—an understanding markedly determined by the Counter-Reformation mentality. In the effort to straighten out the domestic chaos of many years' brewing, Trent had underscored the authoritative and disciplinary aspects of Catholicism. The priests produced by its seminaries were a corps of loyal, obedient men trained spiritually and intellectually to form the type of Catholic called for by the rigorous letter and spirit of the Council.

The 20th century, however, has witnessed a renewed understanding of the Church. For many years now, ideas apparently long forgotten have found their way back into the minds of Catholics the world over. The freedom of the individual Christian, rooted in his personal dignity and in his baptismal consecration to Christ; the priestly character of the entire People of God; the co-responsibility of all Catholics for building up the body of Christ—these and other truths are reshaping our understanding of the Church of Jesus Christ. A new age in the Church has in truth begun. The seminary preparing men to be ministers in today's Church must necessarily be "a new kind of seminary".

The *Decree on Priestly Training* promulgated by Pope Paul VI on October 28, 1965 is a relatively brief document. It is a solidly good one, however, for it embodies principles which, if imaginatively and energetically acted upon, can create seminaries equal to the challenge before them in the post-conciliar period that has just begun.

Though short, the Decree has had a long and complicated history. It may be of service to some readers to indicate the principal stages in the genesis of this document.

During the period of preparation prior to the Council, the Preparatory Commission on Studies and Seminaries had drawn up two separate but related schemata. One was a Constitution, "On Forming Seminarians", the other a Decree, "On Fostering Ecclesiastical Vocations". The former— and principal—document consisted of six chapters which covered the whole range of seminary formation, including the important area of post-ordination education.

At a meeting of the Pontifical Central Commission held in February, 1962, the decision was made to insert the Decree on vocations into the Constitution on seminaries as its first chapter. This was done, and the resulting document was sent to the bishops of the world. However, the text did not come up for discussion during the first session of the Council in the fall of 1962. Nevertheless, written comments and suggestions for improvement were sent into the newly formed Conciliar Commission on Seminaries, Studies, and Catholic Schools throughout this period.

In the spring of 1963 the Conciliar Commission thoroughly revised and shortened the schema drawn up by the Preparatory Commission, in light of the suggestions it had received. The new text was sent to the bishops in May of that year, shortly before the death of Pope John. During October and November of the second session of the Council, the seminary commission again reexamined the

text. Three subcommissions were formed to eval-
uate the suggestions that had come in during the
preceding five months, and the entire commission
reworked the document once more.

Some of the criticisms leveled against the
schema are interesting to note. Many bishops declared the text to be either completely or partly
unacceptable. They thought it failed to propose
sufficiently radical changes in the seminary system,
and that it did not make adequate allowance for
the legitimate differences in seminary life that
should be permitted in various parts of the world.
Some also found it wanting because of its failure
to stress the need for the seminarian's personal
responsibility for his intellectual, spiritual and pastoral formation. Finally, many complained of
what they considered the dry, juridical and some-
what negative tone of the document. After further
revision, the text was again submitted to the bishops for their criticism and comment. As yet,
however, the schema had not come up for debate
on the floor of the Council. This was the situation
at the end of the second session.

After all this work, it must have come as something of a blow when, in January, 1964, the Coordinating Committee of the Council decided, in
the interests of time, to reduce a number of
schemata to simple lists of propositions to be presented to the fathers of the Council for their approval (or rejection) but not for debate. The
seminary schema was one such document. During
March of 1964, the seminary commission, having
already emended the text of the schema in light
of the bishops' criticisms, drew from it nineteen
summary propositions. These were later expanded
to twenty-two. It was in this form that the schema

finally came to the floor of the Council during the third session. Contrary to the original intention of the Coordinating Committee, it was, happily, the object of a lively and sharp debate among the bishops.

Between the third and fourth sessions, the saga of the schema came full circle, for it was once more given the status of a full-dress document (albeit a shorter one than first planned) with the rank of "Decree" rather than that of "Constitution". This was the text that was approved by the Council during its last session and promulgated by Pope Paul on October 28, 1965.

"The Council is fully aware that the desired renovation of the whole Church depends upon a priestly ministry animated by the spirit of Christ." The brief introductory paragraph of the Decree clarifies both the place of the document in the entire teaching and movement of Vatican Council II and the governing purpose which determined its composition. It states principles designed to preserve proper continuity with sound seminary formation of the past, and at the same time it provides necessary and healthy adaptations for the spirit of the Council and the changed conditions of our times. Directly, the text envisages the diocesan priest. At a deeper level, however, its principles call for adaptation by all priests, diocesan and religious, of every rite.

I

Priestly Training in Different Countries

One of the clearly acknowledged principles of Vatican Council II is that general laws should be

sensitively adapted to fit local conditions. Unity does
not mean uniformity. In this regard earlier documents such as the *Constitution on the Church*
and the *Constitution on the Sacred Liturgy* had
done pioneer work in enunciating a principle
that has application in every sphere in the
Church's life. The present Decree on seminaries,
by calling for an organized program of priestly
studies under the guidance of episcopal conferences, issues a sharp challenge to the bishops of
the world to assume proper leadership in the formation of a clergy equal to the pastoral needs of
the people they serve. So much will depend, in
practice, upon the manner in which the conferences of bishops function during the next decade
or so. It is within their power to introduce creative and far-reaching changes in this crucial area
of priestly formation, as in so many others.

II
More Intensive Fostering of Priestly Vocations

Underlying the teaching of the Council on vocations is a twofold conviction. On the one hand,
God will never cease to sow the seeds of a vocation in the hearts of a sufficient number of young
men; on the other hand, he wills to bring those
seeds to growth and full flowering through the
instrumentality of men. That is his way with us.
The responsibility for encouraging vocations to
the priesthood rests upon the whole Christian
community. While, according to the Decree, modern, planned techniques should be used in the
effort to promote vocations, the primary and indispensable means must always be the "fully
Christian life" in which young men grow up:

hence, the insistence of the Decree that the most important agents in the fostering of vocations are Christian families and parishes, *"in whose abundant life* the young people themselves take an active part"* (emphasis added). Much is said at present about the shortage of vocations in many parts of the world. The surest way to overcome this difficulty is so to form families and parish communities with the spirit of Christ that contact with them will mean an experience of integral Christianity. There are seldom adequate substitutes for these primary "seminaries" in the Church.

It is interesting to note that the Decree treats minor seminaries at the end of this general section on the fostering of vocations. During the discussions at the Council there was a considerable difference of opinion among the bishops on the subject of minor seminaries. Many wished a strong statement affirming their necessity. The majority, however, preferred to avoid taking such a position. Consequently, the Decree skirts the issue and settles for some important recommendations for minor seminaries, where they exist. Behind the words of the document is the evident serious concern of the bishops that minor seminaries provide a normal, healthy formation for adolescents and that nothing be introduced into the program that would in the least way run counter to the norms of sound psychology. Especially noteworthy, too, is the declaration that the "the parents, too, playing their appropriate part" is a needed factor in a well-planned minor seminary. Adolescence is a crucial period in the development of young persons everywhere. The Church may not, in conscience, bypass any help that can be obtained to make the formation of adolescent seminarians as balanced and perceptive as possible.

III

Major Seminaries

The Council had no hesitation about affirming the necessity of major seminaries (traditionally this has been a six-year program in most countries, embracing the last two years of undergraduate college work and the four years of properly theological training). In the clearest terms the Decree enunciates the governing thesis of the rest of the document: *"The whole training of the students should have as its object to make them true shepherds of souls after the example of our Lord Jesus Christ, teacher, priest and shepherd"* (emphasis added). This pastoral orientation is to be the one criterion of the spiritual, intellectual and disciplinary components of seminary life. The People of God needs wise and holy pastors. It is the seminary's task, under God, to prepare men for this ministry of service.

It is not surprising, then, that the Decree has specific directives concerning the choice of seminary professors and administrators. They are to be chosen from among "the best" men the Church can find. In preparation for their task, they are to receive a solid doctrinal formation, suitable pastoral experience and a special spiritual and and pedagogical training. The implementation of this directive calls for great wisdom and breadth of vision on the part of bishops and communities engaged in seminary work. Nothing less would be worthy of the grave responsibility that is theirs.

The example, too, of a seminary faculty, which

"should cultivate the closest harmony of spirit and action" forming with the students "such a family as corresponds to our Lord's prayer 'that they may be one'", will contribute incalculably to the formation of fine priest-servants of the Church. The ideal put to seminary faculties is a frightening one. This Decree (n. 5) provides them with thoughts for long and sober reflection.

What the Council says about the entire process of selecting and testing students for the priesthood is governed by a twofold concern: a due firmness, in view of the heavy responsibility of the pastoral ministry, and a constant solicitude for the integral personal formation of the seminarians. Bishops are urged not to lower their standards "notwithstanding the regrettable shortage of priests". Similarly, they should not fear to combine seminaries for the sake of providing a better total education for their candidates for the priesthood. Where there are seminaries with rather large enrollments, however, there should be, within the one community, some sort of breakdown into smaller groups of students so that "better provision will be made for the solid training of the students". However excellent their academic advantages, large seminaries must not become "priest factories". Even the very physical shape and arrangement of seminary buildings is an important factor in promoting the familial sense of which the Council speaks.

IV

Greater Attention to Spiritual Training

The spiritual formation of seminarians should be in close harmony with their doctrinal and pastoral formation. This is the first principle stated in this section of the Decree. A priest must be an integral man. His personal response to God in prayer, of whatever sort, should harmonize with his intellectual grasp of the Christian message and with the pastoral orientation of his life. Among other things this demands that the spiritual program of the seminary be in full accord with the contemporary biblical, theological and liturgical movements that are the inspiration and source (it is to be hoped) of the seminarian's academic formation. What takes place in chapel must dovetail with the intellectual activities of the classroom. Both must make sense in light of the apostolate and the pastoral ministry.

Briefly, the Council wishes seminarians to be men of profound Christian piety and positive maturity. They themselves must grow on the very bread which they are to break for their people. Union with Christ in the mystery of his death and resurrection; the Gospel ideal of charity; the mystery of the Church; the manifold presence of Christ in Word, sacrament, and fellowman: these truths and realities, the stuff of all authentic Christian living, must, *a fortiori*, be assimilated into the spiritual bloodstream of those who aspire to serve the People of God.

Seminarians are also to be mature men, aware of the responsibilities they shall assume. In the Western Church this will mean, in particular, both a realistic and a spiritual attitude toward celibacy. Sheer physical removal from the world and from many of the more obvious enticements to sin is no preparation for the positive commitment of celibacy. Nor is an ignorance of, or a disparaging attitude toward, the excellence of the sacrament of matrimony. Celibacy, as Auxiliary Bishop Reuss of Mainz remarked at the Council, is not "a sort of admission ticket to holy orders". It is a pre-eminently positive reality. The seminarian is not merely renouncing something. Still less is he renouncing *love*. What he is doing·is renouncing *a way of loving* for the sake of the kingdom of heaven. Given the fact that it appears altogether unlikely that we may expect any change in the discipline of celibacy in the Western Church in the near future, an enormous burden rests upon those in authority to help candidates for the priesthood live celibate lives in such a positive and loving way "that not only will their daily conduct and activities suffer no harm from celibacy, but they themselves will acquire greater mastery of mind and body, grow in maturity and receive a greater measure of the blessedness promised by the Gospel". It is not enough to reaffirm the rule of celibacy in idealistic terms or to condemn those who question its validity. All the resources at our disposal—doctrinal, spiritual and psychological—must be marshaled to enable men called to the priesthood to receive celibacy "as a precious gift of God".

Only after the Decree has spoken at some length about the sort of spirituality that should characterize the priest does it bring up the question of discipline in the seminary. Discipline is not an end in itself. It is seen by the Council, however, as an important means toward the formation of mature, responsible priests. The question of obedience is being aired at the moment in writings and in discussions at every level. We are far from a perfect theology of obedience that will reconcile the apparent antinomies of rightful authority and personal freedom. Nor does this Decree or any other document of Vatican Council II give us the final answer. However, we are asked to approach a solution with intelligence, responsibility, a spirit of faith and a sensitivity to the good of the whole community.

It is much easier to talk of maturity in the seminary than to produce mature priests. The seminary system to date has not been altogether successful in helping many seminarians achieve a due measure of maturity by the time of ordination. Freed from the immediate practical responsibilities that must be shouldered by their peers in the world, seminarians, through little or no fault of their own, are not infrequently lacking in maturity at the end of their course of studies. Of great significance, therefore, is the provision (n. 12) whereby bishops may take certain practical steps to ensure greater maturity on the part of ordinands. These may include such measures as an extended period of pastoral work after a certain point in the seminarians' theological formation or, should this be judged necessary, the raising of the minimal age for priestly ordination, with the possible exercise of the order of deacon for a length of time before promotion to priesthood. Once again we see a recognition by Vatican Council II that unity is not to be confused with uniformity, and that those in charge of local dioceses are to be presumed competent to decide what specific adaptations of general law are needed in their own territories.

V
The Revision of Ecclesiastical Studies

The following section on intellectual formation in the seminary begins with a statement that has often been made by popes during the past thirty or more years. Before beginning the study of theology, seminarians should "already have received that literary and scientific education which is a prerequisite to higher studies in their own countries". In the United States and in many other parts of the world today, it is becoming increasingly difficult to assume that this test will be met and automatically passed with flying colors. In particular, the seminary program at the college level must be reviewed. However excellent the courses, can seminary college faculties by themselves provide the type of liberal education the Council envisages? Oftentimes two or three professors (or less) constitute an entire department, whether of English, history, science or philosophy. In such cases it is simply impossible to offer that variety of teaching personnel which is in itself a significant part of a liberal education. However the solution may vary in different circumstances, the seminary college program can continue to operate in isolation only at its own risk.

The second general principle concerning seminary studies is likewise of considerable moment. Philosophy and theology must be integrated more closely and consistently so that both help to provide the seminarian with a mature appreciation of the mystery of Christ. In the past, the two years of philosophical training, during which scant mention would be made in the classroom of matters supernatural or Christian, tended to create in the minds of the students a rationalistic outlook that ill prepared them for the true study of theology. There was just a bit of truth in the irreverent remark that these were the "pagan years" in seminary training. It is noteworthy, then, that the Decree enjoins an introductory course in the mystery of salvation from the outset of the major seminary. Such a course could help noticeably to give an integral and thoroughly Christian orientation to the entire major seminary program.

Several significant points are also made about the approach to the teaching of philosophy itself. To be sure, the Council wishes the seminarian's philosophical studies to give him a sound, coherent and rational interpretation of reality. However, it does not wish to turn the young student into a complacent "answer-man" who thinks he has all the "reasonable" solutions to the mystery of life. A sense of awe and of mystery should be the result of any honestly taught course in philosophy—or in any other discipline, for that matter.

Finally, the injunction that "careful attention should be paid to the bearing of philosophy on the real problems of life, as well as to the questions that engage the minds of the students" suggests that a reevaluation of the content of the traditional philosophy course is in order. It may well prove that we have been carrying an amount of obsolete baggage for some time now. To be honest, the philosophy program should be freed from the burden of attempting to cover the whole range of speculative problems concerning man and his place in the universe. The day should likewise long since have passed when we looked upon philosophy primarily as the "handmaid of theology" furnishing the future theologian with a correct and useful speculative vocabulary.

Far-reaching directives are likewise given concerning the teaching of the theological sciences. The following propositions summarize the main points of the Council's teaching:

1. The theological sciences should be so taught that Catholic doctrine will truly be the food of the seminarian's own life and, by his ministry, the nourishment of his people.

2. Particular care should be given to the study of the Bible, which must be the soul of all theology.

3. Dogmatic or doctrinal theology is to be taught thematically: *i.e.,* the key concepts of revelation should be presented in their historical development, beginning from the Scriptures and continuing through their unfolding in the life of the Church.

4. Theology must be taught so that the mysteries of salvation will be seen to be relevant to the pressing issues of today.

5. The other theological disciplines, especially moral theology, should also be renewed "through a more vivid contact with the mystery of Christ and the history of salvation".

6. Seminarians should be led to a fuller understanding of other Christian Churches in order to prepare them for the ecumenical task embraced by the Council.

7. Seminarians should also have a suitable knowledge of non-Christian religions, in view of their pastoral ministry.

8. Teaching methods and the whole program of studies should be revised so as to serve more effectively the "true and intimate formation of the students".

9. Finally, especially promising students should be given the chance to pursue special studies to "meet the various needs of the apostolate".

Some words of comment on the third of these propositions. The manner in which dogmatic theology is to be taught is of immense significance. If followed, the directives of the Decree should produce something of a revolution in seminary theological training. For years the customary way of teaching theology was according to the thesis method. Each treatise in dogma (*e.g.*, redemption, grace, the Trinity) was made up of a number of *logically ordered* theses or propositions which affirmed in Scholastic terms a precise aspect of Catholic doctrine. There then followed the "proof" of the thesis, usually drawn from Scripture, tradition and reason. The Bible was used, as were the Fathers of the Church, but neither source was studied for its own sake. Quotations from St. Paul, St. John, St. Augustine and St. Jerome would be cited to back up the thesis in question. Undoubtedly, the method had certain advantages. It provided an orderly and exact synthesis of doctrine and it trained young theologians in accurate thinking. In the hands of an intelligent and sensitive teacher the method could and did produce well-informed theological students. *But it had one enormous disadvantage:* it was *a-historical.* The theses in a given tract of theology and the use that was made of biblical and patristic sources gave no adequate understanding of the slow and often complicated historical development of a seed-idea (as found in Scripture) into a carefully elaborated declaration of pope or council. This lack of an historical sense is perhaps the major weakness of Catholic theology today. At times it makes extremely difficult the acceptance of so-called "new ideas" which, apart from an awareness of doctrinal development, appear to threaten "traditional" Catholic teaching. We can understand, then, the capital importance of the Council's directive that dogmatic theology is to be taught thematically according to the historical development of the Church's understanding of the mysteries of salvation.

Virtually all manuals of theology, therefore, are officially obsolete by the force of this statement of the Council. At the moment a vacuum has been created, for there is little material to replace the traditional textbooks. Meanwhile, a certain amount of responsible experimentation would seem necessary before we can expect a selection of theological textbooks that represent more than a superficial compliance with the directives of the Council.

What, one may ask, is the attitude of the conciliar Decree toward the study of St. Thomas in Catholic seminaries? Clearly, the Council had no intention of repudiating the high and repeated words of praise for the Angelic Doctor on the part of the highest ecclesiastical authorities over the centuries. On the other hand, the mention of St. Thomas in the text of this Decree is a modest one. In the paragraph which speaks of the need for a thematic and historical approach to theology, the text states that the students should learn to penetrate speculatively the mysteries of salvation "with St. Thomas as teacher". The place of St. Thomas in seminary theological training did not go unmentioned on the floor of the Council. On the contrary, it was the object of one of the sharpest debates during the third session. A strong and vocal minority complained bitterly of the scant mention made of St. Thomas in the schema. Others took a quite opposite stand. It was on this occasion

that Cardinal Léger made the famous remark: "Woe
to the Church of one teacher!" He had strongly
objected to Thomistic theology being the only
theology taught in seminaries, and he insisted that it
was the *person* and the honest, open, *intellectual
attitude* of the great Doctor, rather than his system
as such, that should be the perennial model and
inspiration for theologians.

The words of the Decree concerning the ecumenical formation of candidates for the priesthood are brief but they need to be underscored.
Ecumenism should not be looked upon as a
peripheral movement in the Church to which
certain priests, by reason of background or temperament, may be attracted. Rather, it is an existen-
tial dimension of Christianity itself which colors
and affects the Church in all its activities. There
is no area of Catholicism—whether it be liturgy,
the apostolate, missionary activity or the theological disciplines—where the Church is not weakened
and impoverished by the tragedy of divided Chris-
tendom. Consequently, an ecumenical sensitivity
and concern must permeate the Church at every
level. This will not be the case, however, no matter how much goodwill is expended, if there is not
a *"fuller understanding* of the Churches and ecclesial communities separated from the Holy See"
(emphasis added). Separated Christians cannot
love one another as Christ intends unless they first
know one another.

How is ecumenical understanding to be
brought about? At the academic level the seminarian must be offered the opportunity to study
at some length the theological positions of other
Christian Churches. Desirably, this would mean
that specific courses, given by Catholic *and non-*

Catholic theologians as well, would be a normal part of undergraduate seminary training. Catholic priests do not have to be specialists in Protestant or Orthodox theology, but they should be sufficiently well-informed so as to be able to enter intelligently and sympathetically into conversation with clergymen and theologians of other Christian communions.

Knowledge of ideas is not enough, however. It is not theological systems which are separated but *communities of persons:* hence the great importance of frequent and regular contact between Catholic and non-Catholic seminarians during the years of theological training. Experience has already shown the value of these personal contacts in preparing seminarians for ecumenical work in the ministry. It is to be hoped that the beginnings that have been made in this area will be promoted and developed as an official part of seminary training from now on.

Again, the recommendation (n. 17) that there should be a thoroughgoing revision of the whole program of theological training, both as to method and content, presents no small challenge to seminary educators. It is one thing to point out the deficiencies of the present system; it is quite another to come up with an alternate program that is clearly a marked improvement. Here, as elsewhere, we need responsible experimentation and the widest possible exchange of ideas among the members of a single faculty and among the various seminaries of the world, especially those of the same nation or territory.

Finally, the recommendation that young men of superior talent be given the opportunity to pursue special studies should be understood and in-

terpreted in the broadest way possible. It is not
merely a question of preparing a certain number
of priests to fill the official posts of a diocese
(chancery office or social service), however necessary these works may be. Rather it is to be hoped
that there will be formed a growing corps of highly
trained priests in a diocese who will be able to
fill a variety of posts in various areas of the apostolate. Newman centers, adult education programs,
ecumenical endeavors and similar projects are instances that come to mind. Serious historians feel
that one of the major contributing factors both
to the Reformation and to the grave setback to the
Church in France in the last century was the
failure of the Church to meet the intellectual challenge of the day. We can ill afford to fail again.

VI

The Promotion of Strictly Pastoral Training

The Decree insisted at the outset of its reflec-
tions and directives that the entire orientation of
seminary life must be pastoral. Nevertheless, there
is that special aspect of preparation for the
priesthood that may be called strictly pastoral
training. The Council makes the obvious declaration that the candidate for the priesthood should
have previous instruction in the specific pastoral
functions he is to perform; that he should have a
genuine solicitude for all persons coming under
his care; and that he be made aware of the findings of contemporary social and allied sciences
which would make his pastoral ministry more
effective. But perhaps the most important recommendation is the general directive that semina-

rians are to grow in such capabilities as "the willingness to listen to others and the capacity to open their hearts in a spirit of charity to the various needs of their fellowmen". The priest must be not only a wise teacher of men but also a patient, compassionate and reverent listener.

The final directive in this section has to do with the initiation of seminarians into pastoral work during the course of the school year as well as during the time of vacations. "You need a swimming pool to learn how to swim," remarked Cardinal Suenens during the third session of the Council, when this point was being discussed. In the John XXIII Seminary, founded by the cardinal, the carefully planned active apostolate of the seminarians is considered as essential a part of their preparation for the priesthood as the intellectual and directly spiritual formation that is offered. In many seminaries in the United States students have long been engaged in a good measure of active apostolic work during their course of training. It is not so much a question, then, of increasing the amount of time spent in apostolic work as it is of planning and assessing this activity more critically. It is essential that the administration recognize the intrinsic importance of this part of a seminarian's formation and that it continually strive to make it more effective. Here, too, the very physical location of a seminary is an important factor in the sort of apostolic work open to the seminarians. While existing seminaries cannot be transplanted at will, new ones should not be so located as to suggest that the major concern of the authorities is to preserve seminarians from the contagion of this world. "Prophylactic training", to use the phrase of Archbishop Giovanni

Colombo of Milan, is hardly in accord with the spirit of Vatican Council II.

VII
Later Studies

The Decree here returns to a point which it had already touched upon in part: the post-ordination education of the clergy. The text has in mind all the clergy without exception. Relatively few may be chosen to go on for graduate studies, strictly so called, but all, young and old, need the help of a program of continuing education throughout their pastoral ministry. The *Decree on the Ministry and Life of Priests* also insists on this fact. National conferences of bishops must take seriously their responsibility to make use of the most suitable means at their disposal to provide for the ongoing education of the clergy. Fortunately, good beginnings, by way of summer institutes for priests, have already taken firm root in the United States and elsewhere. However, they need to be multiplied many score so that it will be relatively easy for priests everywhere to avail themselves of the opportunity to grow in their understanding of the Christian mystery and of its application to all the areas of their pastoral ministry.

Conclusion

The bishops at Trent were well aware of the significance of the step they had taken, during the last months of the Council, in calling for the establishment of seminaries in all the dioceses of the world. Rightly did they judge that it would be the Tridentine seminary which would be the most effective instrument in implementing the decrees of the Council. History proved them correct. The fathers of Vatican Council II have entertained similar hopes. During the four sessions of the Council of *aggiornamento* virtually every aspect of the Church's life and of its relations with others was subject to long and hard scrutiny. As a result we now possess a corpus of conciliar teaching which is a clear and unambiguous summons to renewal and reform. Among the documents of the Council some stand out as veritable giants, strong in vision and mighty in their power to bring to realization the hopes of the saintly old man who first dreamed the dream of a new Pentecost in our day. But the greatest of conciliar declarations is utterly powerless unless priests in the years to come understand the message of Vatican Council II and are willing to spend themselves unsparingly in its implementation. That is why so much depends upon the enlightened interpretation and fulfillment of this brief Decree. Intelligence, patience, humility, faith—and good humor—must all be marshaled in the momentous and exciting cause of the renewal of priestly training. May the Lord have compassion upon the vessels of clay at his disposal and use them to his honor and glory.

Decretum
De Institutione Sacerdotale

DECREE ON
PRIESTLY TRAINING*

**Promulgated by Pope Paul VI
October 28, 1965**

* The *Decree on Priestly Training* was translated by the Reverends B. Hayes, S.M., S. Fagan, S.M. and Austin Flannery, O.P.

PAUL BISHOP

DECREE ON
PRIESTLY TRAINING

Introduction

The Council is fully aware that the desired renewal of the whole Church depends in great part upon a priestly ministry animated by the spirit of Christ[1] and it solemnly affirms the critical impor-

---

[1] It is clear from the words by which our divine Lord appointed the apostles, with their successors and fellow workers, to be the preachers of the Gospel, the leaders of the new chosen people and the dispensers of the mysteries of God, that according to the will of Christ himself the progress of the whole People of God depends in the highest degree on the ministry of priests. This is supported by the statements of the Fathers and saints and by a whole series of papal documents. Cf. especially St. Pius X, Exhortation to the Clergy *Haerent animo,* Aug. 4, 1908: *S. Pii X Acta,* IV (1908), pp. 237-64; Pius XI, Encyclical Letter *Ad catholici sacerdotii,* Dec. 20, 1935: *A.A.S.* 28 (1936), esp. pp. 37-52; Pius XII, Apostolic Exhortation *Menti nostrae,* Sept. 23, 1950: *A.A.S.* 42 (1950), pp. 657-702; John XXIII, Encyclical Letter *Sacerdotii nostri primordia,* Aug. 1, 1959: *A.A.S.* 51 (1959), pp. 545-79; Paul VI, Apostolic Letter *Summi Dei Verbum,* Nov. 4, 1963: *A.A.S.* 55 (1963), pp. 979-95.

tance of priestly training. It lays down certain
fundamental principles, wherein regulations already tested by the experience of centuries are
reaffirmed and new regulations are introduced, in
harmony with the constitutions and decrees of the
sacred Council and the changed conditions of our
times. Because of the unity of the Catholic priesthood, this priestly formation is required for all
priests, secular, religious and of every rite. Hence,
although these directives are immediately concerned with the diocesan clergy, they should with
due qualification be adapted to all.

I

Priestly Training in Different Countries

1. Since only regulations of a general nature
can be made, owing to the wide diversity of peoples
and countries, each nation or rite should have its
own *Program of Priestly Training*. This should be
drawn up by the episcopal conference,[2] should be
revised at regular intervals and approved by the
Holy See. In every such program, the general regulations will be adapted to the circumstances of
time and place, so that priestly training will always answer the pastoral requirements of the particular area in which the ministry is to be exercised.

---

[2] The whole course of priestly training—i.e., the organization of the seminary, spiritual formation, course of studies,
the common life and rule of the students, and pastoral practice—should be adapted to local conditions. The general principles of this adaptation should be decided by episcopal
conferences for the diocesan clergy and in a similar manner
by the competent superiors for religious (cf. the General
Statutes attached to the Apostolic Constitution *Sedes sapientiae*, n. 19).

II

More Intensive Fostering of Priestly Vocations

2. The duty of fostering vocations[3] falls on the whole Christian community and they should discharge it principally by living fully Christian lives. The greatest contribution is made by families which are animated by a spirit of faith, charity and piety and which provide, as it were, a first seminary, and by parishes in whose abundant life the young people themselves take an active part. Teachers and all who are in any way involved in the education of boys and young men—and this applies especially to Catholic associations—should endeavor to train the young entrusted to them to recognize a divine vocation and to follow it willingly. All priests should show their apostolic zeal by fostering vocations as much as possible, and should draw the hearts of young men to the priesthood by the example of their humble, hardworking and happy lives, as well as by their mutual charity and fraternal cooperation.

It is the duty of bishops to encourage their people to foster vocations, and to see that all their energies and undertakings are closely coordi-

---

[3] Almost everywhere one of the chief anxieties of the Church today is the dearth of vocations. Cf. Pius XII, Apostolic Exhortation *Menti nostrae*, Sept. 23, 1950: *A.A.S.* 42 (1950), p. 682: "Both in Catholic countries and in mission territories, the number of priests is insufficient to cope with the increasing demands." Also cf. John XXIII, Allocution *To the First International Congress on Religious Vocations,* Dec. 16, 1961: *L'Osservatore Romano,* Dec. 17, 1961: "The problem of ecclesiastical and religious vocations is a daily preoccupation with the Pope. . . . Vocations are the object of his prayer, the ardent longing of his soul."

nated, sparing themselves no sacrifice in their efforts to help, as fathers, those who in their judgment have been called to God's service.

Such active collaboration by all God's people in the task of fostering vocations is a response to the action of divine providence, which endows with appropriate qualities and helps with divine grace those who have been chosen by God to share in the hierarchical priesthood of Christ. Divine providence entrusts to the lawful ministers of the Church the task of judging the suitability of candidates seeking this exalted office with right intention and full liberty, and, after they have been approved, of calling and consecrating them with the seal of the Holy Spirit to the worship of God and the service of the Church.[4]

The Council, first of all, recommends the traditional aids toward this general cooperation, such as unceasing prayer,[4a] Christian penance and progressively more advanced instruction for the faithful, wherein the necessity, nature and excellence of the priestly vocation will be set forth by preaching, catechetics and the various means of social communication. The Council also directs that the organizations for promoting vocations which have been— or are about to be—set up in the various dioceses, regions or countries, in accordance with the pertinent pontifical documents, should coordinate and systematize all pastoral work for vocations and develop them with as much discretion as zeal,

---

[4] Cf. Pius XII, Apostolic Constitution *Sedes sapientiae,* May 31, 1956: *A.A.S.* 48 (1956), p. 357; Paul VI, Apostolic Letter *Summi Dei Verbum,* Nov. 4, 1963: *A.A.S.* 55 (1963), pp. 984ff.

[4a] This could also be rendered "fervent prayer" (*instans oratio*) . Several translators have given that rendering. (Translator's footnote)

making full use of the aids provided by modern psychological and sociological teaching.[5]

The work of fostering vocations should be done generously. It should cross the boundaries of individual dioceses, countries, religious congregations and rites and, with the needs of the universal Church in view, should assist especially those areas for which workers are required with special urgency for the Lord's vineyard.

3. In minor seminaries founded to nurture the seeds of vocation, students should be prepared by a special religious formation and, especially, by suitable spiritual direction, to follow Christ the redeemer with generous souls and pure hearts. Under the fatherly supervision of the superiors—the parents, too, playing their appropriate part—let them lead lives suited to the age, mentality and development of young people. Their way of life should be fully in keeping with the standards of sound psychology and should include suitable experience of the ordinary affairs of daily life and contact with their own families.[6] Furthermore, all that is laid down in the following paragraphs for major seminaries should be adapted to the

---

5 Cf. especially Pius XII, Motu Proprio *Cum nobis,* on the establishment of the pontifical work for priestly vocations, Nov. 4, 1941: *A.A.S.* 33 (1941), p. 479, together with the attached statutes and rules promulgated by the Sacred Congregation for Seminaries and Universities, Sept. 8, 1943; Pius XII, Motu Proprio *Cum supremae,* on the pontifical work for religious vocations, Feb. 11, 1955: *A.A.S.* 47 (1955), p. 266, together with the attached statutes and rules promulgated by the Sacred Congregation for Religious (*ibid.,* pp. 298-301) ; Vatican Council II, *Decree on the Renewal of Religious Life,* Oct. 28, 1965, n. 24; Vatican Council II, *Decree on the Pastoral Office of Bishops in the Church,* Oct. 28, 1965, n. 15.

6 Cf. Pius XII, Apostolic Exhortation *Menti nostrae,* Sept. 23, 1950: *A.A.S.* 42 (1950) , p. 685.

minor seminary also as far as is suitable to its purpose and character. Courses of studies should be so arranged that pupils may be able to continue them elsewhere without inconvenience, should they embrace another state of life.

The same care should be taken to foster the seeds of vocations in those special institutes which, in keeping with local conditions, take the place of minor seminaries, and also among boys educated in other schools or according to other systems. Colleges for late vocations and other undertakings for the same purpose should be diligently promoted.

III

Major Seminaries

4. Major seminaries are necessary for priestly training. In them the whole training of the students should have as its object to make them true shepherds of souls after the example of our Lord Jesus Christ, teacher, priest and shepherd.[7] Hence, they should be trained for the ministry of the Word, so that they may gain an ever increasing understanding of the revealed Word of God, making it their own by meditation, and giving it expression in their speech and in their lives. They should be trained for the ministry of worship and sanctification, so that by prayer and the celebration of the sacred liturgical functions they may carry on the work of salvation through the eucharistic sacrifice and the sacraments. They should be trained to undertake the ministry of the shepherd, that they

---

[7] Cf. **Vatican Council II**, *Dogmatic Constitution on the Church,* Nov. 21, 1964, n. 28: *A.A.S.* 57 (1965), p. 34.

may know how to represent Christ to men, Christ who "has not come to be served, but to serve, and to give his life as a ransom for many" (Mark 10, 45; John 13, 12-17), and that they may win over many by becoming the servants of all (1 Cor. 9, 19).

Hence, all the elements of their training, spiritual, intellectual, disciplinary, should be coordinated with this pastoral aim in view, and all superiors and teachers should zealously cooperate to carry out this program in loyal obedience to the bishop's authority.

5. The training of students depends not only on wise regulations but also, and especially, on competent educators. Seminary superiors and professors should therefore be chosen from among the best[8] and should receive a careful preparation in sound doctrine, suitable pastoral experience and special training in spirituality and teaching methods. To provide this training, special colleges should be established, or at least suitable courses should be organized, as well as regular meetings of seminary directors.

Superiors and professors should be keenly aware of the extent to which their mental outlook and conduct affects the formation of their students. Under the guidance of the rector they should cul-

---

[8] Cf. Pius XI, Encyclical Letter *Ad catholici sacerdotii*, Dec. 20, 1935: *A.A.S.* 28 (1936), p. 37: "In the first place let careful choice be made of superiors and professors. . . . Give these sacred colleges priests of the greatest virtue, and do not hesitate to withdraw them from tasks which indeed seem to be of greater importance but which cannot be compared with this supremely important matter, the place of which nothing else can supply." This principle of choosing the best men for the seminaries is again insisted upon by Pius XII in his Apostolic Letter *To the Hierarchy of Brazil*, April 23, 1947: *Discourses and Radio Messages of His Holiness Pius XII*, IX, pp. 579-80.

tivate the closest harmony of spirit and action, and should form with one another and with the students such a family as corresponds to our divine Lord's prayer: "That they may be one" (cf. John 17, 11), and quickens in the students' hearts a sense of joy in their vocation. With his constant and affectionate interest, the bishop should encourage those engaged in seminary work and show himself a true father in Christ to the students. Furthermore, all priests should regard the seminary as the very heart of the diocese and give it their willing support.[9]

6. Each candidate should be subjected to vigilant and careful inquiry, keeping in mind his age and development, concerning his right intention and freedom of choice, his spiritual, moral and intellectual fitness, adequate physical and mental health, and possible hereditary traits. Account should also be taken of the candidate's capacity for undertaking the obligations of the priesthood and carrying out his pastoral duties.[10]

Notwithstanding the regrettable shortage of priests,[11] due strictness should always be brought to bear on the choice and testing of students. God will not allow his Church to lack ministers if the worthy are promoted and those who are not suited to the ministry are guided with fatherly kindness

---

[9] With regard to this general duty of priests to give their support to seminaries, cf. Paul VI, Apostolic Letter *Summi Dei Verbum*, Nov. 4, 1963: *A.A.S.* 53 (1963), p. 984.

[10] Cf. Pius XII, Apostolic Exhortation *Menti nostrae*, Sept. 23, 1950: *A.A.S.* 42 (1950), p. 684; cf. also the Sacred Congregation for the Sacraments, Letter to Bishops *Magna equidem*, Dec. 27, 1935, n. 10. For religious, cf. the General Statutes attached to the Apostolic Constitution *Sedes sapientiae*, May 31, 1956, n. 33. Also cf. Paul VI, Apostolic Letter *Summi Dei Verbum*, Nov. 4, 1963: *A.A.S.* 55 (1963), pp. 987f.

[11] Cf. Pius XI, Encyclical Letter *Ad catholici sacerdotii*, Dec. 20, 1935: *A.A.S.* 28 (1936), p. 41

and in due time to adopt another calling. These should be directed in such a way that, conscious of their Christian vocation, they will zealously engage in the lay apostolate.

7. Where individual dioceses are unable to provide adequate separate seminaries out of their own resources, common seminaries should be established and maintained. These common seminaries could meet the needs of a group of dioceses or of an entire region or nation. By their means better provision will be made for the solid training of the students, which is of paramount importance in this matter. These seminaries, regional or national, are to be controlled according to regulations drawn up by the bishops concerned,[12] and approved by the Holy See.

In large seminaries, the students should be suitably organized in smaller groups, to enable more personal attention to be given to each student, while retaining unity of discipline and scientific training.

IV

Greater Attention to Spiritual Training

8. Spiritual formation should be closely associated with doctrinal and pastoral formation, and, the spiritual director especially lending his assistance,[13] should be conducted in such a way that

---

[12] It is decreed that, in drawing up the statutes of regional or national seminaries, all bishops concerned will take part, setting aside canon 1357, par. 4, of the Code of Canon Law.

[13] Cf. Pius XII, Apostolic Exhortation *Menti nostrae,* Sept. 23, 1950: *A.A.S.* 42 (1950), p. 674; Sacred Congregation of Seminaries and Universities, *La formazione spirituale del candidato al sacerdozio:* Vatican City, 1965.

the students may learn to live in intimate and unceasing union with God the Father through his
Son Jesus Christ, in the Holy Spirit. Those who
are to take on the likeness of Christ the priest by
sacred ordination should form the habit of drawing
close to him as friends in every detail of their
lives.[14] They should live his paschal mystery in
such a way that they will know how to initiate
into it the people committed to their charge. They
should be taught to seek Christ in faithful meditation on the Word of God and in active participation in the sacred mysteries of the Church,
especially the eucharist and the divine office,[15]
to seek him in the bishop who gives them their
mission, and in the people to whom they are sent,
especially the poor, little children, the weak, sinners and unbelievers. With the confidence of sons
they should love and reverence the most blessed
Virgin Mary, who was given as a mother to the
disciple by Jesus Christ as he was dying on the
cross.

The exercises of piety commended by the venerable practice of the Church should be strongly
encouraged, but care must be taken that spiritual
formation does not consist in these alone, or merely
develop religious sentiment. The students should

---

14 Cf. St. Pius X, Exhortation to the Clergy *Haerent animo*,
Aug. 4, 1908: *S. Pii X Acta,* IV, pp. 242-44; Pius XII, Apostolic
Exhortation *Menti nostrae*, Sept. 23, 1950: *A.A.S.* 42 (1950),
pp. 659-61; John XXIII, Encyclical Letter *Sacerdotii nostri
primordia*, Aug. 1, 1959: *A.A.S.* 51 (1959), pp. 550f.

15 Cf. Pius XII, Encyclical Letter *Mediator Dei*, Nov. 20,
1947: *A.A.S.* 39 (1947), pp. 547ff., 572f.; John XXIII, Apostolic
Exhortation *Sacrae laudis*, Jan. 6, 1962: *A.A.S.* 54 (1962), p.
69; Vatican Council II, *Constitution on the Sacred Liturgy*,
Dec. 4, 1963, nn. 16-17: *A.A.S.* 56 (1964), pp. 104f.; Sacred
Congregation of Rites, *Instructio ad exsecutionem Constitutionis de Sacra Liturgia recte ordinandam*, Sept. 27, 1964, nn.
14-17: *A.A.S.* 56 (1964), pp. 880f.

learn, rather, to live according to the standard of the Gospel, to be firmly established in faith, hope and charity, so that the practice of these virtues may develop in them a spirit of prayer,[16] strengthen and protect their vocation and invigorate their other virtues, intensifying their zeal for winning all men to Christ.

9. The students should be thoroughly penetrated with a sense of the mystery of the Church, which this holy Council has set particularly in relief. Their sense of the Church will find expression in a humble and filial attachment to the vicar of Christ and, after ordination, in their loyal cooperation with the bishop, in harmony with their fellow priests. By this means they will bear witness to that unity which draws men to Christ.[17] They should learn to participate with enthusiasm in the life of the Church as a whole, keeping in mind the words of St. Augustine: "A man possesses the Holy Spirit in the measure in which he loves the Church." [18] Students must clearly understand that it is not their lot in life to lord it over others and enjoy honors, but to devote themselves completely to the service of God and the pastoral ministry. With special care they should be so trained in priestly obedience, poverty and a spirit of self-denial,[19] that they may accustom themselves to live

---

[16] Cf. John XXIII, Encyclical Letter *Sacerdotii nostri primordia*, Aug. 1, 1959: *A.A.S.* 51 (1959), pp. 559f.

[17] Cf. Vatican Council II, *Dogmatic Constitution on the Church*, Nov. 21, 1964: *A.A.S.* 57 (1965), pp. 35f.

[18] Cf. St. Augustine, *In Ioannem tract.*, 32, 8: *P.L.* 35, 1646.

[19] Cf. Pius XII, Apostolic Exhortation *Menti nostrae*, Sept. 23, 1950: *A.A.S.* 42 (1950), pp. 662f., 685, 690; John XXIII, Encyclical Letter *Sacerdotii nostri primordia*, Aug. 1, 1959: *A.A.S.* 51 (1959), pp. 551-53, 556f.; Paul VI, Encyclical Letter *Ecclesiam suam*, Aug. 6, 1964: *A.A.S.* 56 (1964), pp. 634f.; Vatican Council II, *Dogmatic Constitution on the Church*, Nov. 21, 1964, esp. n. 8: *A.A.S.* 57 (1965), p. 12.

in conformity with the crucified Christ and to give up willingly even those things that are lawful but not expedient.

Students should be informed of the obligations they are undertaking, and no difficulty of the priestly life should be concealed from them. They should not, however, be almost completely taken up with the element of danger in their future apostolate, but should rather be trained to strengthen their spiritual life as fully as possible in the very exercise of their pastoral activity.

10. Students who follow the venerable tradition of priestly celibacy as laid down by the holy and permanent regulations of their own rite should be very carefully trained for this state. In it they renounce marriage for the sake of the kingdom of heaven (cf. Matt. 19, 12) and hold fast to their Lord with that undivided love[20] which is profoundly in harmony with the new covenant; they bear witness to the resurrection in a future life (cf. Luke 20, 36)[21] and obtain the most useful assistance toward the constant exercise of that perfect charity by which they can become all things to all men in their priestly ministry.[22] They should keenly realize with what sense of gratitude they should embrace this state, not only as a precept of ecclesiastical law, but as a precious gift of God which they should ask for humbly and to which they should hasten to respond freely and generously, under the inspiration and with the assistance of the Holy Spirit.

20 Cf. Pius XII, Encyclical Letter *Sacra virginitas,* March 25, 1954: *A.A.S.* 46 (1954), pp. 165ff.

21 Cf. St. Cyprian, *De habitu virginum,* 22: *P.L.* 4, 475; St. Ambrose, *De virginibus* I, 8, 52: *P.L.* 16, 202f.

22 Cf. Pius XII, Apostolic Exhortation *Menti nostrae,* Sept. 23, 1950: *A.A.S.* 42 (1950), p. 663.

Students should have a proper knowledge of the duties and dignity of Christian marriage, which represents the love existing between Christ and the Church (cf. Eph. 5, 32). They should recognize the greater excellence of virginity consecrated to Christ,[23] however, so that they may offer themselves to the Lord with a fully deliberate and generous choice, and a complete surrender of body and soul.

They should be put on their guard against the dangers which threaten their chastity, especially in present-day society.[24] They should learn how, with suitable natural and supernatural safeguards, to weave their renunciation of marriage into the pattern of their lives, so that not only will their daily conduct and activities suffer no harm from celibacy, but they themselves will acquire greater mastery of mind and body, will grow in maturity and receive a greater measure of the blessedness promised by the Gospel.

11. The standards of Christian education should be faithfully maintained and they should be supplemented by the latest findings of sound psychology and pedagogy. A prudent system of training will therefore aim at developing in the students a proper degree of human maturity. This will be chiefly attested by a certain stability of character, the ability to make carefully weighed decisions, and a sound judgment of events and people. The students should learn self-control,[24a]

---

23 Cf. Pius XII, Encyclical Letter *Sacra virginitas,* March 25, 1954: *A.A.S.* 46 (1954), pp. 170-74.

24 Cf. Pius XII, Apostolic Exhortation *Menti nostrae,* Sept. 23, 1950: *A.A.S.* 42 (1950), pp. 664, 690f.

24a The Latin of the phrase is: *"Alumni propriam indolem recte componere assuescant."* Translators seem divided as to the exact meaning of the words. Some take it, as we have

develop strength of character, and in general value those good qualities which are esteemed by men and make Christ's minister acceptable.[25] Such qualities are sincerity, a constant love of justice, fidelity to one's promises, courtesy in deed, modesty and charity in speech.

The discipline of seminary life should be regarded not only as a strong protection for community life and charity, but as a necessary part of the complete system of training. Its purpose is to inculcate self-control, to promote solid maturity of personality and the formation of those other traits of character which are most useful for the ordered and fruitful activity of the Church. But it should be applied in such a way as to develop in the students a readiness to accept the authority of superiors out of deep conviction—because of the dictates of their conscience, that is to say (cf. Rom 13, 5)—and for supernatural reasons. Standards of discipline should be applied with due regard for the age of the students, so that while they gradually acquire self-mastery, they will at the same time form the habit of using their freedom with discretion, of acting on their own initiative and energeti-

---

done, to refer to self-control—thus the translation published in French by Editions du Cerf: *"Que les seminaristes prennent l'habitude de dominer leur temperament."* However, others take it to refer to the students' development of their abilities —thus the translation edited by Fr. Walter M. Abbott, S.J., in *The Documents of the Christian Church:* "They should be practiced in an intelligent organization of their proper talents," and that published by the English Catholic Truth Society: "The students should know how to make the most of their own abilities," and the Italian translation published by *L'Osservatore Romano: "Gli alunni si abituino a perfezionare come si deve la propria indole."* (Translator's footnote)

[25] Cf. Paul VI, Apostolic Letter *Summi Dei Verbum,* Nov. 4, 1963: *A.A.S.* 55 (1963), p. 991.

cally,[26] and of working harmoniously with their confreres and with the laity.

The whole program of the seminary should be so organized that, with its atmosphere of piety and silence and its concern for mutual cooperation, it should already be an initiation to the students' future lives as priests.

12. To provide a more solid foundation for the students' spiritual formation, and enable them to decide upon their vocation with full deliberation, it will rest with the bishops to set apart a suitable interval of time for a more intensive spiritual preparation. It is for them also to consider carefully the advantage of arranging some interruption of studies, or of providing suitable training in pastoral work, so that better provision can be made for testing the fitness of candidates for the priesthood. It will be for the bishops likewise, keeping in mind the special conditions of each country, to determine if the age at present required by the common law for the reception of sacred orders should be raised, and to discuss whether it be opportune to make a ruling that at the end of the theological course students should work for a time as deacons before being raised to the priesthood.

V

The Revision of Ecclesiastical Studies

Before seminarians commence their specifically ecclasiastical studies, they should already have received that literary and scientific education which is a prerequisite to higher studies in their own

[26] Cf. Pius XII, Apostolic Exhortation *Menti nostrae,* Sept. 23, 1950: *A.A.S.* 42 (1950), p. 686.

countries. In addition they should acquire a knowledge of Latin which will enable them to understand and make use of so many scientific sources and of the documents of the Church.[27] The study of the liturgical language of their own rite should also be considered a necessity and the acquisition of an adequate knowledge of the languages of Holy Scripture and tradition should be warmly encouraged.

14. In the revision of ecclesiastical studies the main object to be kept in mind is a more effective coordination of philosophy and theology so that they supplement one another in revealing to the minds of the students with ever increasing clarity the mystery of Christ, which affects the whole course of human history, exercises an unceasing influence on the Church, and operates mainly through the ministry of the priest.[28]

This vision should be communicated to the students from the very first moment of their training; their ecclesiastical studies, therefore, should begin with an introductory course of appropriate duration. In this course the mystery of salvation should be presented in such a way that the students may understand the meaning, arrangement and pastoral aim of ecclesiastical studies, and may be helped at the same time to make faith the foundation and inner principle of their entire personal lives, and be strengthened in their resolve to accept their vocation with joyful heart and complete personal dedication.

15. Philosophical subjects should be taught in

---

27 Cf. Paul VI, Apostolic Letter *Summi Dei Verbum,* Nov. 4, 1963: *A.A.S.* 55 (1963), p. 993.

28 Cf. Vatican Council II, *Dogmatic Constitution on the Church,* Nov. 21, 1964, nn. 7, 28: *A.A.S.* 57 (1965), pp. 9-11, 33f.

such a way as to lead the students gradually to a solid and consistent knowledge of man, the world and God. The students should rely on that philosophical patrimony which is forever valid,[29] but should also take account of modern philosophical studies, especially those which have greater influence in their own country, as well as recent progress in the sciences. Thus, by correctly understanding the modern mind, students will be prepared to enter into dialogue with their contemporaries.[30]

The history of philosophy should be taught in such a manner that students may grasp the fundamental principles of the various systems, retaining those elements which are proved to be true, while being able to detect and refute those which are false.

The teaching method adopted should stimulate in the students a love of rigorous investigation, observation and demonstration of the truth, as well as an honest recognition of the limits of human knowledge. Careful attention should be paid to the bearing of philosophy on the real problems of life, as well as to the questions that engage the minds of the students. The students themselves should be helped to perceive the connection between philosophical arguments and the mysteries of salvation which theology considers in the higher light of faith.

16. Theological subjects should be taught in the light of faith, under the guidance of the magisterium of the Church,[31] in such a way that students

---

[29] Cf. Pius XII, Encyclical Letter *Humani generis*, Aug. 12, 1950: *A.A.S.* 42 (1950), pp. 571-75.

[30] Cf. Paul VI, Encyclical Letter *Ecclesiam suam*, Aug. 6, 1964: *A.A.S.* 56 (1964), pp. 637ff.

[31] Cf. Pius XII, Encyclical Letter *Humani generis*, Aug. 12, 1950: *A.A.S.* 42 (1950), pp. 567-69; Pius XII, Allocution *Si*

will draw pure Catholic teaching from divine revelation, will enter deeply into its meaning, make it
the nourishment of their spiritual life,[32] and learn
to proclaim, explain, and defend it in their
priestly ministry.

Students should receive a most careful training
in Holy Scripture, which should be the soul, as it
were, of all theology.[33] After a suitable introductory course, they should receive an accurate initiation in exegetical method. They should study
closely the principal themes of divine revelation
and should find inspiration and nourishment in
daily reading and meditation upon the sacred
books.[34]

The following order should be observed in the
treatment of dogmatic theology: biblical themes
should have first place; then students should be
shown what the Fathers of the Church, both of the
East and of the West, have contributed toward
the faithful transmission and elucidation of each of
the revealed truths; then the later history of

---

diligis, May 31, 1954: *A.A.S.* 46 (1954) , pp. 314f.; Paul VI,
Allocution delivered at the Pontifical Gregorian University,
March 12. 1964: *A.A.S.* 56 (1964) , pp. 364f.; Vatican Council
II, *Dogmatic Constitution on the Church,* Nov. 21, 1964, n. 25:
A.A.S. 57 (1965), pp. 29-31.

[32] Cf. St. Bonaventure, *Itinerarium mentis in Deum,* Prol.,
n. 4: "Let no one think he will find sufficiency in a reading
which lacks unction, an inquiry which lacks devotion, a search
which arouses no wonder, a survey without enthusiasm, indus-
try without piety, knowledge without love, intelligence without humility, application without grace, contemplation without wisdom inspired by God": St. Bonaventure, *Opera Omnia,*
V (Quaracchi, 1891) , p. 296.

[33] Cf. Leo XIII, Encyclical Letter *Providentissimus Deus,*
Nov. 18, 1893: *A.A.S.* 26 (1893-94) , p. 283.

[34] Cf. Pontifical Biblical Commission, *Instructio de Sacra
Scriptura recte docenda,* May 13, 1950: *A.A.S.* 42 (1950), p. 502.

dogma, including its relation to the general history of the Church;[35] lastly, in order to throw as full a light as possible on the mysteries of salvation, the students should learn to examine more deeply, with the help of speculation and with St. Thomas as teacher, all aspects of these mysteries, and to perceive their interconnection.[36] They should be taught also to discern these mysteries as they are present and effective at all times in the ceremonies of the liturgy,[37] and in the whole life of the Church. They should learn to seek the solution of human problems in the light of revelation, to apply its eternal truths to the changing conditions of human affairs, and to express them in language

---

[35] Cf. Pius XII, Encyclical Letter *Humani generis*, Aug. 12, 1950: *A.A.S.* 42 (1950), pp. 568f.: "The sacred sciences are being constantly rejuvenated by the study of their sacred sources, while on the other hand that speculation which neglects the deeper examination of the sacred deposit becomes sterile, as we know from experience."

[36] Cf. Pius XII, Address *To Seminarians*, June 24, 1939: *A.A.S.* 31 (1939), p. 247: "Emulation in seeking and propagating the truth is not suppressed, but is rather stimulated and given its true direction by commending the teaching of St. Thomas." Also cf. Paul VI, Address delivered at the Pontifical Gregorian University, March 12, 1964: *A.A.S.* 56 (1964), p. 365: "Let [teachers] listen with respect to the Doctors of the Church, among whom St. Thomas holds the principal place. For so great is the power of the Angelic Doctor's genius, so sincere his love of truth, and so great his wisdom in investigating the deepest truths, in illustrating them and linking them together with a most fitting bond of unity, that his teaching is a most efficacious instrument, not only for safeguarding the foundations of the faith, but also in gaining the fruits of healthy progress with profit and security." Cf. also Paul VI, Allocution *To the Sixth International Thomistic Congress*, Sept. 10, 1965.

[37] Cf. Vatican Council II, *Constitution on the Sacred Liturgy*, Dec. 4, 1963, nn. 7, 16: *A.A.S.* 56 (1964), pp. 100f., 104f.

which people of the modern world will understand.[38]

In like manner the other theological subjects
should be renewed through a more vivid contact
with the mystery of Christ and the history of salvation. Special care should be given to the perfecting
of moral theology. Its scientific presentation should
draw more fully on the teaching of Holy Scripture
and should throw light upon the exalted vocation
of the faithful in Christ and their obligation to
bring forth fruit in charity for the life of the
world. In the same way the teaching of canon law
and Church history should take into account the
mystery of the Church, as it was set forth in the dogmatic constitution, *De Ecclesia,* promulgated by this
Council. Sacred liturgy, which is to be regarded as
the first and indispensable source of the true Christian spirit, should be taught as prescribed in arti-
cles 15 and 16 of the *Constitution on the Sacred
Liturgy.*[39]

With due regard to the conditions of different
countries, students should be introduced to a fuller
understanding of the Churches and ecclesial communities separated from the Holy See, so that
they may be able to take part in promoting the
restoration of unity among all Christians according to the decisions of the Council.[40]

They should also be introduced to a knowledge

38 Cf. Paul VI, Encyclical Letter *Ecclesiam suam,* Aug. 6,
1964: *A.A.S.* 56 (1964), pp. 640f.

39 Cf. Vatican Council II, *Constitution on the Sacred
Liturgy,* Dec. 4, 1963, nn. 10, 14-16; Sacred Congregation of
Rites, *Instructio ad exsecutionem Constitutionis de Sacra Liturgia recte ordinandam,* Sept. 26, 1964, nn. 11-12: *A.A.S.* 56
(1964), pp. 879f.

40 Cf. Vatican Council II, *Decree on Ecumenism,* Nov. 21,
1964, nn. 1, 9-10: *A.A.S.* 57 (1965), pp. 90, 98f.

of whatever other religions are most commonly encountered in this or that region, so that they may recognize more clearly how much goodness and truth they possess through the providence of God, and learn how to refute their errors and bring the light of truth to those who are without it.

17. Doctrinal training should not have the mere communication of ideas as its objective, but a genuine and profound formation of the students. Teaching methods, consequently, should be revised. This applies to lectures, discussions and seminars and involves encouraging the students themselves to study, whether privately or in small groups. Great care should be taken to achieve an overall training which is coherent and solid, avoiding over-multiplication of subjects and lectures and omitting problems which have little importance today or which should be left to higher academic studies.

18. It is the bishops' responsibility to send young men of suitable character, virtue and ability to special institutes, faculties or universities, so that the various needs of the apostolate may be met by priests trained to a higher scientific standard in the sacred sciences and in other appropriate subjects. But the spiritual and pastoral training of these young men, especially if they have not yet been raised to the priesthood, should by no means by neglected.

VI
The Promotion of Strictly Pastoral Training

19. The pastoral preoccupation which should characterize every feature of the students' train-

ing[41] also requires that they should be carefully instructed in all matters which are especially relevant in the sacred ministry. These are, principally, catechetics, preaching, liturgical worship and the administration of the sacraments, works of charity, their duty to contact those in error and the unbelievers, and other pastoral duties. They should receive precise instruction in the art of directing souls. They will thus be able, first of all, to form all the members of the Church in a way of life which is fully and consciously Christian and apostolic. They will also instill in them a sense of the obligation of fulfilling the duties of their state. With equal solicitude they should learn how to help religious men and women to persevere in the grace of their vocation and to make progress, according to the spirit of their respective institutes.[42]

---

[41] The perfect ideal of the pastor can be seen in the recent papal documents dealing specifically with the life, qualities and training of priests. Cf. especially St. Pius X, Exhortation to the Clergy *Haerent animo*, Aug. 4, 1908: *S. Pii X Acta*, IV, pp. 237ff.; Pius XI, Encyclical Letter *Ad catholici sacerdotii*, Dec. 20, 1935: *A.A.S.* 28 (1936), pp. 5ff.; Pius XII, Apostolic Exhortation *Menti nostrae*, Sept. 23, 1950: *A.A.S.* 42 (1950), pp. 657ff.; John XXIII, Encyclical Letter *Sacerdotii nostri primordia*, Aug. 1, 1959: *A.A.S.* 51 (1959), pp. 545ff.; Paul VI, Apostolic Letter *Summi Dei Verbum*, Nov. 4, 1963: *A.A.S.* 55 (1963), pp. 979ff. Much information about pastoral training is also given in the encyclicals *Mystici corporis* (1943), *Mediator Dei* (1947), *Evangelii praecones* (1951), *Sacra virginitas* (1954), *Musicae sacrae disciplina* (1955), *Princeps pastorum* (1959), and (for religious) in the Apostolic Constitution *Sedes sapientiae* (1956). Pius XII, John XXIII and Paul VI have often thrown light on the ideal of the good shepherd in their allocutions to seminarians and priests.

[42] As regards the importance of that state which is set up by the profession of the evangelical counsels, cf. Vatican Council II, *Dogmatic Constitution on the Church,* Nov. 21, 1964, ch. VI: *A.A.S.* 57 (1965), pp. 49-53; also cf. Vatican Council II, *Decree on the Renewal of Religious Life,* Oct. 28, 1965.

In general those aptitudes should be cultivated in the students which are most conducive to dialogue among men. They include the willingness to listen to others and the capacity to open their hearts in a spirit of charity to the various needs of their fellowmen.[43]

20. They should be taught to use correctly the aids provided by pedagogy, psychology and sociology,[44] in keeping with the regulations of ecclesiastical authority. They should also be carefully taught how to inspire and encourage apostolic action among the laity,[45] and to promote various and more effective forms of apostolate; and they should be filled with that truly Catholic spirit which habitually looks beyond the boundaries of diocese, country or rite, to meet the needs of the whole Church, being prepared in spirit to preach the Gospel everywhere.[46]

21. Students must learn the art of exercising the apostolate not only in theory but in practice and should be able to act on their own initiative and in cooperation with others. To this end, they should be initiated to pastoral work as a part of their course of studies, and also in holiday time, in suitable undertakings. These enterprises should be carried out methodically and under the direction of experts in pastoral work, according to the prudent judgment of the bishops, taking into account the age of the students and local conditions, and al-

---

[43] Cf. Paul VI, Encyclical Letter *Ecclesiam suam*, Aug. 6, 1964: *A.A.S.* 56 (1964), *passim*, esp. pp. 635f., 640ff.

[44] Cf. especially John XXIII, Encyclical Letter *Mater et Magistra*, May 15, 1961: *A.A.S.* 53 (1961), pp. 401ff.

[45] Cf. especially Vatican Council II, *Dogmatic Constitution on the Church*, Nov. 21, 1964, n. 33: *A.A.S.* 57 (1965), p. 39.

[46] Cf. Vatican Council II, *Dogmatic Constitution on the Church*, Nov. 21, 1964, n. 17: *A.A.S.* 57 (1965), pp. 20f.

ways keeping in mind the outstanding power of supernatural helps.[47]

VII
Later Studies

22. Since priestly training, especially in view of the circumstances of modern society, should be continued and perfected after the completion of the seminary course,[48] it will be the task of episcopal conferences in each country to provide the appropriate means for its continuation. Examples of such means are: pastoral institutes cooperating with certain parishes selected for the purpose, the holding of meetings at stated times, and suitable projects by which the junior clergy will be gradually introduced to priestly life and apostolic activity in their spiritual, intellectual and pastoral aspects, with opportunities for constant renewal and progress.

---

[47] Very many papal documents sound a warning against the danger of neglecting the supernatural goal in pastoral activity and of minimizing the value of supernatural means, at least in practice; cf. especially the documents recommended in footnote 41.

[48] More recent documents of the Holy See urge that special attention be paid to newly ordained priests. The following are especially recommended: Pius XII, Motu Proprio *Quandoquidem*, April 2, 1949: *A.A.S.* 41 (1949), pp. 165-67; Pius XII, Apostolic Exhortation *Menti nostrae*, Sept. 23, 1950: *A.A.S.* 42 (1950); Pius XII, Apostolic Constitution *Sedes sapientiae* (for religious), May 31, 1956, with the General Statutes attached to it; Pius XII, Address *To the Priests of the "Convictus Barcinonensis"*, June 14, 1957: *Discourses and Radio Messages of His Holiness Pius XII*, XIX, pp. 271-73; Paul VI, Address *To the Priests of the Gian Matteo Giberti Institute of the Diocese of Verona*, March 11, 1964.

Conclusion

The fathers of the Council, continuing the work begun by the Council of Trent, confidently entrust to superiors and professors in seminaries the duty of training Christ's future priests in the spirit of the renewal promoted by the Council itself. At the same time, they most strongly exhort those who are preparing for the sacred ministry to develop a keen awareness that the hopes of the Church and the salvation of souls are being committed to them, and urge them by their joyful acceptance of the regulations in this Decree to bring forth most abundant and lasting fruit.

* * *

Each and every point stated in this Decree has satisfied the fathers of the sacred Council. And we, by the authority bestowed on us by Christ, together with the venerable fathers, approve it in the Holy Spirit, we decree it and we enact it; and we order the promulgation, to God's glory, of what has been enacted synodically.

Rome, in St. Peter's Basilica, October 28, 1965

Paul, Bishop of the Catholic Church
(The fathers' signatures follow)

Study-Club Questions

1. Why are the family and the parish the most important agents in the fostering of vocations to the priesthood?

2. Why do you think the Council skirted the issue of affirming the necessity of minor seminaries?

3. What ideal does the Decree put to seminary faculties?

4. What twofold principle does the Decree suggest for the entire process of selecting and testing students for the priesthood?

5. Why should the spiritual formation of seminarians be in close harmony with their doctrinal and pastoral formation?

6. How can seminarians develop a realistic and spiritual attitude toward celibacy?

7. What suggestions does the Decree (n. 12) provide to ensure greater maturity on the part of the ordinands?

8. Why does the Decree insist on a solid program of philosophical studies for the seminarian?

9. Mention some far-reaching directives contained in the Decree concerning the teaching of theology.

10. Mention some advantages and disadvantages of the traditional method of teaching dogmatic theology.

11. What is the attitude of the conciliar Decree toward the study of St. Thomas in Catholic seminaries?

12. How important is the ecumenical formation of candidates for the priesthood?

13. Why should seminarians be initiated into pastoral work during the course of the school year as well as during vacation time?

14. How important is the post-ordination education of the clergy?

15. Why does Vatican Council II seek to create a new kind of seminary in the Church today?

16. Can you suggest some creative and far-reaching changes in this crucial area of priestly formation?

17. Mention some possible explanations for the present-day shortage of vocations to the priesthood.

18. Why must the spiritual, intellectual and disciplinary components of seminary life have a pastoral orientation?

19. What qualifications does the Decree suggest for the selection of seminary faculties?

20. What are some of the advantages and disadvantages of large seminaries?

21. Why must the spiritual program of a seminary be in full accord with the contemporary biblical, theological and liturgical movements?

22. What is the virtue of obedience? How should it be exercised by the priest, the religious and the laity?

23. Do you think the minimal age for priestly ordination should be raised?

24. Why should we not look upon philosophy primarily as the "handmaid of theology"?

25. For the welfare of the Church, how much depends on the enlightened interpretation and fulfillment of this Decree?

Decree on the Ministry and Life of Priests

Commentary

INTRODUCTION

From the moment the work of preparation for Vatican Council II began, it was clear that the roles of bishops and of laymen would receive major attention on the conciliar agenda. It has been a commonplace in recent years to observe that the teaching of Vatican Council I on the primacy and infallibility of the bishop of Rome seriously needed to be complemented by a more developed doctrine of the episcopate. Only against such a perspective could papal primacy ever be rightly understood. If Vatican Council II were to discuss anything of a dogmatic nature, surely it would attempt to right the imbalance created by the unfinished character of the teaching of Vatican Council I (1869-1870).

In addition, one could easily surmise that the laity would receive a fair measure of consideration at the forthcoming Council. The development of Catholic Action and other forms of the lay apostolate since World War I made it a foregone conclusion that Vatican Council II would at least corroborate by its teaching the advances in the theology of the laity that had been made during the past decades.

The simple priest, or "presbyter" as he is called in ecclesiastical Latin (the word is simply a transliteration of the Greek term for "elder"), turns out to be something of a forgotten man in this picture. Yet how could one permanently ignore the crucial role played by the priest in the daily life of the Church? As the *de facto* liaison between bishop and people, he performs a task that, for good or ill, greatly affects the vitality of the Church as it is concretely embodied in the local parish or in specialized communities of Catholics (schools, seminaries and religious institutions of whatever sort). The present conciliar document is an attempt to speak specifically and practically about that enormous corps of Catholic men upon whom the Church will always depend so heavily for its well-being and effectiveness.

Taken in isolation, the *Decree on the Ministry and Life of Priests* would probably not be considered one of the outstanding documents of the Council. The cautiousness and lack of clarity it exhibits in certain sections leaves one a bit unsatisfied; so, too, the rather long list of moral exhortations tend to pall the modern reader. In brief, the text by itself lacks the incisiveness and verve that one would perhaps hope for in a statement of this sort.

However, the Decree must not be viewed in isolation. Its brief introduction indicates that the present document is to be read in light of the total conciliar teaching, especially in relation to such key documents as the *Constitution on the Sacred Liturgy,* the *Constitution on the Church,* the *Decree on the Pastoral Office of the Bishops in the Church* and the *Decree on Priestly Training,* which together offer considerable teaching on the priesthood.

A word, finally, about the genesis of the Decree. The original intention of the Conciliar Commission on the Discipline of the Clergy and of the Christian People was to produce a full-fledged schema on the ministry and life of priests that would be debated and voted upon in the usual fashion. In the interim between the second and third sessions of the Council, however, a number of projected documents still in process of formation were, in the interests of time, reduced to a series of propositions or theses to be presented to the bishops for approval (or rejection) but not to be submitted for debate. The present Decree was one such document. In October, 1964, ten propositions on the priestly life (soon expanded to twelve) were presented to the Council fathers. At the insistence of the late Cardinal Meyer of Chicago and others, the proposed draft of propositions was rejected as totally unacceptable. They argued that a full schema with full discussion was demanded by the very nature and importance of the priesthood in the life of the Church. Anything less would be tantamount to an insult to the thousands of Catholic priests throughout the world. Thus there began the work on a full-dress document that finally resulted in the text promulgated by Pope Paul VI in the name of the episcopate on December 7, 1965. Whatever may be the shortcomings of the Decree when viewed in isolation, we must surely be grateful that the bishops of the Council saw to it that their brothers and indispensable collaborators in the ministry were honored by a text whose intention was to treat in serious and expanded fashion the nature and problems of the priestly life.

CHAPTER I
The Priesthood in the Church's Mission

The original draft of the expanded schema was a single chapter with a twofold division. Part I, *The Ministry of Priests,* treated the more properly theological questions of the nature of the priesthood and the functions of the priest in relation to the bishop and to the people. Part II, *The Life of Priests,* dealt with the practical questions of the priest's personal spirituality and the concrete means to solid piety and holiness in the ordained minister of the Church. In the debates during the fourth session, the proposed text was widely criticized by a number of bishops for its lack of organic unity. In particular, Part II was judged to be unrelated to the theological principles contained in Part I. To many this section of the schema appeared to be scarcely more than a lengthy—and rather weary—enumeration of the virtues that should characterize the good and dutiful priest. In an effort to remedy this defect, the Commission recast the text in its present form. Before treating either the ministry or the life of priests (now Chapters II and III respectively), the schema now had a first chapter on the priesthood in the mission of the Church. It was hoped that by situating the priesthood (the order of "presbyters") against the perspective of the total mission of the Church, the text would provide a solid theological foundation for the Council's teaching both on the ministry and on the life of priests.

What can be said by way of commentary on Chapter I? It is a brief chapter, first of all—perhaps too brief. One would wish a slightly more developed treatment, especially since the purpose of the chapter is to lay a sound and unifying foundation for the entire document. Nevertheless, several salient points are made that deserve our close attention.

The opening sentence cannot be meditated upon enough: "The Lord Jesus, 'whom the Father has made holy and sent into the world' (John 10, 36), makes his whole mystical body share in the anointing of the Spirit wherewith he has been anointed" (n. 2). The priestly character of the entire body of Christ is the point of departure for a consideration of the ordained ministry of holy orders. Before we can understand the place of a special way of sharing in the one priesthood of Jesus Christ, we must see and appreciate the priestly character of the whole Church. The "priesthood of all believers" is no metaphor. To be a Christian is to be joined, organically and vitally, to the risen Lord—teacher, worshiper, and shepherd of the new and eternal covenant. To be joined to him is to participate in his threefold priestly office, a role that belongs first to his body as a whole and then to every member of that body. This is the background for any discussion of the ordained ministry of the Church. If there be a priesthood of holy orders, it must be a ministry of service to those who are already a sacred and priestly people.

This is exactly what the Council teaches: "The Lord also appointed certain men as ministers in order that they might be united in one body in which 'all the members have not the same function' (Rom. 12, 4)" (n. 2). There is, indeed, according to traditional Catholic teaching, a divinely intended specialized priestly ministry. Its purpose, however, is solely that of service, "that they might be united in one body". Hierarchy exists for the sake of the community. The priesthood of holy orders exists to build up and strengthen the priesthood of all believers.

A second important truth taught by the Council is that the special or ministerial priesthood is primarily and fully realized in the bishop. For centuries we have tended to define the sacrament of holy orders in terms of the simple priest or "presbyter". Then, almost as though it were an afterthought, we would explain the ministry of the bishop as that of the simple priest with the addition of certain "powers", especially jurisdiction. The "presbyter" and not the bishop was the supposed central figure in the sacrament of orders. Indeed, some theologians even questioned the sacramentality of episcopal consecration.

The teaching of this document and of related conciliar texts is quite the reverse. It is the bishop who is *the* priest (in the ministerial or instrumental sense), and his priesthood is a participation in the threefold ministry of Christ. The simple priest or "presbyter" derives his share in the ministerial priesthood from the bishop. "Because it is joined with the episcopal order, the office of priests shares in the authority by which Christ himself builds up and sanctifies and rules his body" (n. 2). This essential relation of priest to bishop will determine concretely both the wide extent and the limits of the priestly ministry.

The rest of the document will spell out this in detail.

A final key concept in Chapter I is touched upon in paragraph 3: "While being taken from among men and appointed for men in the things that pertain to God so that they may offer gifts and sacrifices for sins, priests live with the rest of men as with brothers." The essential fraternal bond linking priest and people will be dealt with at much greater length in Chapter II. At the outset of the Decree, however, it was thought important to highlight this truth. Priests have indeed been set apart for a specialized ministry in the Church. Their training and, to a large extent, their manner of life (especially in the Western Church) mark them off as "different". The Decree acknowledges this fact but adds: "They would be powerless to serve men if they remained aloof from their life and circumstances" (n. 3). If the fact of priestly ordination so separates a man, psychologically and spiritually, from the people for whose service he is ordained, then the whole purpose of the ministerial priesthood has been undone.

A final word to the reader of this Decree. It may be that he will find Chapter I unsatisfying because of its brevity and a certain lack of orderly and clear development. It is, as we have suggested, a bit too brief. However, the remainder of the Decree will clear up most of the difficulties. A rereading of Chapter I after one has read the entire document may then be more rewarding.

CHAPTER II
The Ministry of Priests

I Functions of Priests

Perhaps the most important doctrinal contribution of the Decree is its description of the priesthood (order of "presbyters") itself in this chapter. For years Catholic theologians were accustomed to define the priesthood in terms of worship and, specifically, of sacrifice. The priest of the new law is the man empowered to offer the sacrifice of the Mass. This view of the priesthood was, and to an extent still is, shared by Catholics generally. Were you to ask a young boy about to enter the seminary why he wished to be a priest, he very likely would reply: "I want to say Mass." It would be much less likely that he would answer: "I want to preach the Gospel."

Vatican Council II has rejected this exclusively cultic or sacrificial view of the priesthood. The "presbyter", as we have already said, derives his share in the special ministry of holy orders from the bishop. The latter, however, is an instrument of Christ in his threefold role of teacher, worshiper ("priest" in the restricted sense), and shepherd. Therefore, the simple priest genuinely participates in each of the bishop's functions. It is altogether insufficient to think of him primarily as a "Mass-priest" and only secondarily as a preacher of the Word of God and a leader of the Christian community.

Chapter II (nn. 4-6) develops at some length the three major functions of the ordained priest. A brief word of commentary about each.

"Since no one can be saved who has not first believed, it is the first task of priests, as co-workers of the bishops, to preach the Gospel of God to all men" (n. 4). From the beginning of its deliberations, Vatican Council II strove to reinstate the Word of God in its rightful position in the life of the Church. Our centuries-old partial neglect of the Word of God in favor of the sacraments has been overcome, at least in principle, by a series of declarations on the importance of Sacred Scripture and the necessity of scriptural preaching. "Word" and "sacrament" belong together. Word without sacrament becomes mere moralizing, or at best the grateful remembrance of saving events of the distant past. Sacrament without Word (the Catholic temptation) begets a view of sacraments bordering on magic. "In the Christian community itself . . . especially for those who seem to have little understanding or belief underlying their practice, the preaching of the Word is required for the sacramental ministry itself, since the sacraments are sacraments of faith drawing their origin and nourishment from the Word" (n. 4). The Decree recalls to us the classic statement of St. Paul: "Faith then depends on hearing, and hearing on the Word of Christ" (Rom. 10, 17).

However, the priest is not just a preacher. Our young boy contemplating the priesthood was not necessarily wrong in giving as his reason for entering the seminary: "I want to say Mass." Properly understood, his reply was a correct one. When the Christian community is assembled to celebrate the eucharist, it realizes most intensely its vocation to be a holy, worshiping People of God. The Council declares: "In the most blessed eucharist is contained the whole spiritual good of the Church, namely Christ himself, our Pasch, and the living bread that gives life to men through his flesh— that flesh which is given life and gives life through

the Holy Spirit. Thus, men are invited and led
to offer themselves, their works and all creation
with Christ. *For this reason, the eucharist appears
as the source and the summit of all preaching of
the Gospel"* (n. 5—emphasis added). Preaching
leads to the action of the holy eucharist. The
eucharist, in turn, sends us forth, both priests and
people, to bear witness by word and example to
the Good News we have received.

The manner in which the Decree treats the
third major function of the priest, that of shepherd, merits our careful attention. No longer is
the burden of emphasis put upon the "power" of
the priest to "rule" the local community. Rather
is it upon his task as *leader* of a family. His role,
it would appear from the Decree, is, above all,
to help others realize their own capacities as free,
mature members of the Church. "It is the priests'
part as instructors of the people in the faith to see
to it, either personally or through others, that each
member of the faithful shall be led in the Holy
Spirit *to the full development of his own vocation
in accordance with the Gospel teaching, and to
sincere and active charity and the liberty with
which Christ has set us free"* (n. 6—emphasis
added). The picture painted is of a priestly minister who, though fully aware of his authoritative
position in the Church, is nevertheless filled with
a keen sense of reverence for the individual persons who form his community.

The priest-leader described in the Decree is,
finally, a man sent to form a genuine Christian
community, one united within itself and embracing in its love and concern the universal
Church. "Priests exercise the function of Christ
as pastor and head in proportion to their share of

authority. In the name of the bishop they gather
the family of God as a brotherhood endowed with
the spirit of unity and lead it in Christ through the
Spirit to God the Father" (n. 6). Christ came to
gather again into a unity the children of God
who had been scattered abroad (cf. John 11,
52). His ministers must continue this task until
he comes.

II Priests' Relations with Others

The Decree next considers, successively, the relations of the priest with his bishop, his fellow-
priests, and his people.

The ministry of the simple priest, we have already seen, is one both of dependence upon, and
fraternal communion with, the ministry of the
bishop. Paragraph 7 develops this idea more fully.
Inherent in the bishop-priest relationship is a sensitive tension. On the one hand, bishops should
not look upon their priests as lackeys existing
only to do their will. On the contrary, they should
"regard them as their indispensable helpers and
advisors in the ministry and in the task of teaching, sanctifying and shepherding the People of
God". The same paragraph declares that bishops
must view their priests as "brothers and friends"
whom they must consult and with whom they
must engage in open and honest dialogue for
the good of the Church. Concretely, the Decree
directs that there should be in each diocese a rep-
resentative body of priests to give the bishop effective assistance in the administration of the diocese.

On the other hand, priests are not independent
agents. Theirs is a position of hierarchical subordination. Further on in the Decree (n. 15), the
question of priestly obedience will be the object
of special consideration. Briefly, and by antici-

pation, the obedience of a priest must be the active virtue of a mature man. Prepared though he may be to accept the final decisions of his legitimate superiors, the priest of this Decree, *in virtue of his very obedience,* does not fear to speak his mind to his bishop about whatever concerns the good of the Church of which both are servants.

To have said this, however, is not to have produced solutions to all practical problems of authority and obedience. How, then, is the tension between genuine episcopal authority and the freedom and responsibility of the priest to be resolved? The Council does not offer a solution directly. However, it does at least suggest, by its repeated insistence in this Decree and elsewhere on the *personal and familial* character of the Church, that the inevitable problems and occasional crises of authority and obedience should be solved not so much by law as by open and frank conversation, by mutual trust and respect, and by a true desire to promote the good of the Church. The responsibility of those in authority to help create such a climate of candor and freedom of expression is a grave one indeed.

The Decree next speaks of the relations between a priest and his fellow priests. The theological basis for the deep unity that should exist among priests is stated in the opening sentence of paragraph 8: "All priests who are constituted in the order of priesthood [*presbyteratus*], by the sacrament of orders are bound together by an intimate sacramental brotherhood; but in a special way they form one priestly body [*presbyterium*] in the diocese to which they are attached under their own bishop." The concept of the priests of a diocese forming a single corporate body (*presbyte-*

rium), collaborating as a team with their bishop whose ministerial priesthood they share, goes back to the earliest days of Christianity when a closely knit body of "presbyters" assisted the bishop in his task of leading and building up the local community. As the Decree points out, the ceremony of ordination has from ancient times (from at least the beginning of the 3rd century) shown that the ordinand is being received into a united brotherhood of priests. Even today, it is a moving sight to see the priests present at an ordination each impose hands upon the ordinands and then gather around the bishop as he recites the consecratory prayer of ordination. It is this sacramental reality that should inspire the practical charity uniting all priests within a diocese, no matter what their age or special ministry. The text cites two problem areas in this regard. The first concerns the relations between diocesan and religious priests. Over the centuries there have been instances of disedifying and scandalous breaches in charity between the diocesan and regular clergy. Fortunately at the present time there are encouraging signs of a renewed understanding, on the part of both groups, of the common bonds that unite them as Christians and as fellow priests and of their common goal: the building up of Christ's body. Here, too, as elsewhere, there can be no real unity in Christ unless there is, first of all, mutual trust and the possibility of frank and honest communication.

The second problem area is, unfortunately, a very real one today: that of the relations between older and younger priests. In many dioceses and religious communities there is a grave threat to the unity of the priestly brotherhood that can do nothing but harm to the Church. Older priests are

tempted to write off the "new breed" clergy as
deficient in good judgment, if not orthodoxy.
Younger priests at times find it all too easy to
dismiss their elders as ill-informed and incompe-
tent in the work of leading the Christian community according to the teachings and spirit of
Vatican Council II. The Decree issues a plea to
both groups for mutual tolerance, respect and understanding. The good of the Church cannot be
served if its priestly ministers have lost that charity for one another that should be the bond of
all Christians.

A final point to be noted is the Council's insistence on the necessity of some sort of common
life among the clergy. Recognizing that widely
different circumstances will dictate different forms
of communal living, the Decree nevertheless lays
down the general principle that priests cannot "go
it alone" either intellectually or spiritually. The
mere fact, too, that the priests of a parish live together under the same roof and share a common
table is no guarantee that there exists a true community of priestly brothers. Finally, the text men-
tions with special praise the various associations
of priests whose purpose it is to encourage holiness in the ministry. Such groups (*e.g.,* the Jesus-
Caritas Union) are doing much in our day to
deepen the bonds of unity and charity among the
brotherhood of priests.

Significant, too, in this conciliar document is
the manner in which the relations between priest
and people are described. Here we touch upon an
area with immense practical implications. However rare the contacts between bishops and the
majority of their flocks, encounters between
priests and people are comparatively frequent. If

nothing else, the faithful at least see and hear their priests in the celebration of the holy eucharist and in the administration of the sacraments. The manner and bearing of priests in such circumstances normally determine in good measure the attitude of the faithful toward their clerical leaders: hence, the importance of the conciliar statement that the fundamental bond linking priest and people is a fraternal one. "Even though the priests of the new law by reason of the sacrament of order fulfill the preeminent and essential function of father and teacher among the People of God and on their behalf, they are, nevertheless, disciples of the Lord along with all the faithful and have been made partakers of the kingdom of God who has called them by his divine grace. *Priests, in common with all who have been reborn in the font of baptism, are brothers among brothers as members of the same body of Christ which all are commanded to build up*" (n. 9—emphasis added).

This last phrase is a further clue to a proper understanding of the priest-people relationship. It is because they share a common responsibility for building up the one body of Christ that priest and people must live and work together in mutual trust and respect. The principle of collegiality affirmed in the *Constitution on the Church* finds application, ultimately, at every level of the Church's life. In the plan of Christ all Christians share a "co-responsibility" for the growth and welfare of the Church and are equipped for this task by their sacramental initiation into the Christian community. Consequently, priests must be sensitive to the voice of God speaking to them and to the Church from the ranks of their brothers of the laity.

Nor is this to be a grudging concession on the part of the clergy. "They should be willing to listen to lay people, give brotherly consideration to their wishes and recognize their experience and competence in the different fields of human activity. In this way they will be able to recognize along with them the signs of the times. While trying the spirits to see if they be of God, they must discover with faith, recognize with joy and foster with diligence the many and varied charismatic gifts of the laity, whether these be of a humble or more exalted kind" (n. 9). Once again the Council asserts, in effect, that the ministry of holy orders exists not to control but to promote creatively the freedom and growth of the individual members of the Christian community.

Perhaps we would not be amiss here to note parenthetically how crucial is the renewal and reform of seminaries in the effective implementation of Vatican Council II. Bishops and priests are the products of a carefully planned and precise program of clerical formation. It is idle to speak glowingly of a fraternal relationship among bishops, priests and people if the schools that prepare men for the ministry reflect another and, in part, a contrary view of the Church and its varied ministries, both lay and clerical. Hence, again, the necessity of understanding and implementing any one document of the Council in light of the entire corpus of conciliar teaching.

III Distribution of Priests; Priestly Vocations

The last section of Chapter II (nn. 10, 11) considers the eminently practical problems of the use of manpower in the priesthood and the recruiting of candidates for the priestly ministry.

It states, in effect, (n. 10), that priests, along

with bishops, have a collegial responsibility for
the good of the entire Church. "Priests should
therefore recall that the solicitude of all the
Churches ought to be their intimate concern"
(n. 10). John Wesley's dictum: "The world is
my parish," should express the mind of every
Catholic priest. While a priest necessarily concen-
trates the brunt of his efforts upon a particular
area or project of the Church, he must not allow himself to become provincial and blinded
to the vision of the universal Church. The number of priests in the United States and elsewhere
who have volunteered for temporary or permanent assignments in Latin America provides an example of what the Council would like to see
encouraged on an even wider scale. Therefore, the
directive of the Decree that the present norms of
incardination and excardination (the canonical
processes, respectively, of receiving one into, and
releasing one from, the service of a particular diocese) should be made more flexible so as to meet
contemporary pastoral needs more effectively.

What the Decree has to say about the urgent
question of priestly vocations is much to the
point. While the Lord will never fail to prepare
a sufficient number for the priesthood, he acts in
this regard as he always does: incarnationally—
through men. The Christian community has the
responsibility of encouraging and developing vocations to the priestly ministry. Above all, this is
an obligation that rests upon those who have already been ordained. How they should fulfill
this serious obligation is carefully described by
the Decree: "In the first place, then, priests are
to make it their most cherished object to make
clear to people the excellence and necessity of
the priesthood. *They do this by their preaching*

*and by the personal witness of a life that shows
clearly a spirit of service and a genuine paschal
joy"* (n. 11—emphasis added). Young men today
are capable of great generosity and sacrifice. They
are idealists as young people have always been.
What they need, by way of stimulus to a priestly
vocation, is the sight of priests whose lives are
being selflessly spent in the service of the Church
and who are themselves filled with that joyous
optimism that is the fruit of a deep faith in the
Easter victory of Jesus Christ. Words of encouragement from such priests cannot fail to bear rich
fruit.

CHAPTER III

The Life of Priests

I Priests' Call to Perfection

Catholics want their clergy to be holy priests—
men of prayer who, open to the inspiration of
the Spirit in their own lives, are thus enabled to
be wise spiritual guides of their fellow Christians.
As would be expected, the present Decree devotes
considerable space—almost the entire third chapter
—to the question of priestly perfection. The first
section of the chapter may be summarized in the
following propositions:

1. In common with all other Christians, priests
share a vocation to perfection.

2. In virtue of their ordination and the sacred actions of their ministry, priests are bound
by yet another title to holiness of life.

3. The exercise of the pastoral ministry should

itself be a most important source of priestly holiness.

4. The evangelical mission of the Church is the norm against which the priest must judge the validity and worth of his many and varied .pastoral activities.

A word of comment on the third of these propositions. Far more important than any specific recommendation for holiness in this Decree is the clear teaching that the priest's way of perfection is the pastoral ministry itself. "Priests will acquire holiness in their own distinctive way by exercising their functions sincerely and tirelessly in the Spirit of Christ" (n. 13). Their active life is not to be thought of as a threat to their life of prayer but rather as a source of their union with Christ. In fact, the demands of the pastoral ministry should provide the primary motivation for priestly asceticism. "As rulers of the community they cultivate the form of asceticism suited to a pastor of souls, renouncing their own convenience, seeking not what is to their own advantage but what will benefit the many for salvation, always making further progress toward a more perfect fulfillment of their pastoral work, and, where the need arises, prepared to break new ground in pastoral methods under the guidance of the Spirit of love who breathes where he wills" (n. 13).

At the turn of the century the French Trappist Jean-Baptiste Chautard taught the important truth that the active apostolate must have its "soul", namely, the prayer-life of the apostle. The present Decree underscores the necessary complementary truth that the apostolate itself is meant to sanctify the apostle and, even more, to make him a man of prayer.

Actually the problem that the priest faces is one of spiritual wholeness and integrity. He is an individual person and as such has a vocation to grow in a relationship with God that is personal and therefore unique. The words of the *Constitution on the Sacred Liturgy* fully apply to him: "The Christian is indeed called to pray with his brethren, but he must also enter into his chamber to pray to the Father in secret" (n. 12). However, he is a churchman, too. He not only leads the community in corporate worship but he must be the first to nourish himself spiritually on the themes and the experience of liturgical prayer. He is, finally, "the man for others", the pastor who finds his joy and strength in his ministry to the brethren. The balanced reconciliation of private prayer, liturgical worship and pastoral service is not an easy thing to achieve in any man's life. However, the earnest priest will persevere in his efforts to do so, for he knows that in each instance he is seeking in faith to find the selfsame Lord, who knows each of us by name, calls us into the unity of his body, and invites us to share in his loving service of mankind. It is the one Christ who gives unity to the many and apparently disparate activities of a priest's life.

The final proposition also merits a brief comment. The problem of how to balance the demands of prayer and reflection, on the one hand, and the increasingly imperious claims upon one's activity, on the other, is felt more acutely by priests today than ever before. There is no simple rule-of-thumb solution. The Decree wisely makes two general but important observations. The first is that the priest must in all things strive to fulfill the will of God. He knows, however, that the divine will is that he should give himself unreservedly to the flock commited to his care. Hence, the very exercise of pastoral charity will be a sanctifying and unifying element in his life. The second observation is that the mission of the Church is the norm for judging the value of one's pastoral activities. Difficult though it may be at times to make such an evaluation, at least an objective norm is given: the evangelical mission of the Church. The Church's mission is that of Christ: to form a community of free and responsible men and women who have themselves joyfully accepted the Father's gift of his Son and who bear witness to others, by word and example, of the transforming power of Christ and of his Spirit. If some of the activities that crowd the schedule of the busy modern priest have little or no connection, even indirectly, with the overall mission of the Church, then they ought to be seriously rethought and ultimately eliminated. It is only when the activities of a priest's life have passed this test of their worth that we may call the exercise of the ministry a positive source of priestly holiness.

II Special Spiritual Requirements in the Life of the Priest

Three special spiritual demands placed upon the priest are next considered by the Decree: obedience, celibacy and the use of material goods.

"Among the virtues especially demanded by the ministry of priests must be reckoned that disposition of mind by which they are always prepared to seek not their own will but the will of him who has sent them" (n. 15). The prerequisite for obedience within the Church is openness to the will of God in all the circumstances of one's life. Within the concrete situation of the priestly ministry, however, such openness to God's will demands sincere obedience to one's superiors, especially one's bishop.

The very nature of the rank of priest or "presbyter" places him in a position of subordination to, and dependence upon, his bishop. Therefore, it is not surprising that the Decree insists upon the obligation of priests to obey their legitimate superiors. What is of special interest, however, is the positive light in which priestly obedience is viewed. Earlier in our commentary, by way of anticipation, we briefly alluded to the teaching of the Council in this section of the Decree. The fathers, in effect, declare that priestly obedience is an active virtue of a mature man. By its very nature it demands personal initiative. Far from merely waiting to receive orders, priests should "be moved by charity to prudently seek new methods of advancing the good of the Church" and should be "insistent to make known the needs of the flock entrusted to them". The priest who never approaches his bishop with new ideas and suggestions but who rather waits passively to be told what to do is not the obedient priest pictured in this Decree. Passive receptivity is not a Christian virtue. Rather, the obedient cleric of this document is one who is actively and energetically concerned for the building up of the body of Christ and who does not fear to speak out honestly and courageously about the steps that should be taken to promote the growth and vitality of the Church of which he, together with his bishop, is the servant and minister.

The teaching on celibacy was the object of great concern at Vatican Council II. The unusually large number of *modi* (specific written recommendations for the improvement of the schema) submitted to the commission concerning paragraph 16 indicates the seriousness with which the subject was taken. Furthermore, the kinds of suggestions and observations show that the question of celibacy is one that raises strong feelings and touches upon deep sensitivities. Briefly the thrust of the conciliar teaching is this:

1. "Perfect and perpetual continence for the sake of the kingdom of heaven" has always been freely embraced by many Christians and is of special value for the priestly life.

2. However, celibacy is not demanded by the nature of the priesthood, as is apparent both from the practice of the early Church (East and West) and from the present practice of the Eastern Churches, which have both a married and a celibate priesthood.

3. Celibacy is especially suitable for the priesthood for two reasons: (a) it is a sign of, and stimulus for, a total dedication to the service of the new humanity brought into being by Christ and the gift of his Spirit; (b) it is a living sign of the world to come "in which the children of the resurrection shall neither be married nor take wives".

4. The Council reaffirms the traditional practice of the Western Church and exhorts the priests who come under its discipline to "cherish their precious gift of priestly celibacy" (n. 16) and to lead lives that will make its practice fruitful for the whole Church.

As is well known, the discussion of whether or not to modify the practice of celibacy in the Western Church was removed from the conciliar agenda in the final session by a decision of Pope Paul (at the request of a certain number of bishops). Moreover, the Pope indicated his intention to reaffirm and, indeed, to strengthen the traditional rule of the Latin Church. At the same time he did not preclude future discussion of the issue, since he indicated his willingness to receive and duly weigh the opinions of his brother-bishops on this important subject. Nevertheless, it is clear that we are not to expect any significant change in the present legislation in the near future.

Therefore, the practical question concerns the way in which celibacy is to be viewed and lived by the priests of the Latin Church. The conciliar text contains some important points for our consideration. Negatively, it should be noted that nowhere does the Decree appeal to purely pragmatic reasons for the maintenance of celibacy. The celibacy envisioned by the Council is not simply chaste bachelorhood embraced for reasons of pastoral efficiency. Neither economic considerations nor the advantages of a readily mobile clerical personnel is a motive cited by the Decree. Rather, celibacy is seen as a gift from God enabling a priest to dedicate himself to his ministry in a qualitatively new way. It is the spiritual good that will accrue to the community thus served—and thus encouraged—that is the real reason for the celibacy of priests. The conclusion should be obvious. Celibacy will "work" only if understood and accepted at a deeply spiritual level. Furthermore, it must be a positive reality in the life of a priest—not the negation of personal love but the channeling of love into new and creative ways of serving and loving the community. Otherwise, celibate priests, for all of their chastity, will be truncated and unfulfilled human beings. Finally, if celibacy is to be seen and embraced in this light, steps must be taken from the outset of one's training for the priesthood to develop the healthiness of outlook, maturity of personality and generosity of spirit that alone can make celibacy a blessing to the priest himself and to the Church.

We cannot read the New Testament honestly without being aware that the Gospel has something to say about the Christian's attitude toward the whole world of creation and the use of temporal goods. In our own day many Christians, lay as well as clerical and religious, are asking probing questions about the place of voluntary poverty in their lives and in the life of the Church. The Decree touches upon this topic. Happily, it begins with a positive affirmation: "By brotherly and friendly association with each other and with other people, priests can learn to cultivate human values and appreciate created goods as gifts of God" (n. 17). There is no place for a negative, Manichean attitude (however subtle) in the heart of a priest. A minister of Jesus Christ, however, must be a *free* man: free from an inordinate concern for material goods and free to obey the promptings of the Holy Spirit in his life. This spiritual freedom and docility cannot normally be achieved without some measure of discipline in the use one makes of created goods. Such is man's weakness and obtuseness that he easily becomes inordinately attached to, and consequently misuses, things excellent in themselves but which have become for him obstacles rather than aids to his union with God. The priest is no exception. He cannot be the totally dedicated servant of the people demanded by his priestly vocation unless he has acquired a genuine spiritual freedom and a healthy sense of detachment.

It is not surprising, therefore, that the Council invites priests to embrace voluntary poverty in imitation of their Lord who, "being rich, became poor for our sakes, that through his poverty we might be rich" (n. 17). Without going into detail, the Decree makes the general observation that "a certain common use of property, like the community of goods extolled in the history of the primitive Church, provides an excellent opening for pastoral charity" (n. 17).

There follows a sober challenge put to bishops and priests: "Guided then by the Spirit of the Lord, who anointed the Savior and sent him to preach the Gospel to the poor, priests and bishops alike are to avoid everything that might in any way antagonize the poor" (n. 17). Fortunately, there are positive signs that some intend to take the Council's invitation to poverty seriously. At the end of the Council a sizable group of bishops who had met during the four sessions to discuss Christian poverty (their number has been variously estimated) issued the following statement: "We renounce forever all appearances and reality of wealth, especially in dress and insignia of precious materials. We will not possess real estate or personal goods or bank accounts. We refuse to be called, either orally or by letter, by titles which signify pomp and power (for example, Eminence, Excellency, Monsignor). We prefer to be called by the evangelical name of 'Father'. We want neither privileges nor priorities."

III Means of Support for Priestly Life

The final section of Chapter III treats certain specific spiritual, intellectual and material means necessary for the proper development and growth of the priestly life.

What the Decree says about the "spiritual

aids" of a priest requires no special comment (n. 18). The exhortation to make use of the standard and tried helps toward spiritual growth is what one would expect in such a document. A priest rapidly discovers in the midst of a busy ministry that he must "make time" for formal prayer if he is going to be able to make of his entire pastoral ministry the way of perfection that it should be.

A few words of comment are in order, however, concerning the Council's observations on the continuing intellectual formation of priests. Long since gone are the days when the priest could be assumed to be the best educated man in his parish. We live in an age of scientific and academic specialization and in a country with increasingly higher standards of education. The priest of today, even in specifically religious matters, is hard put at times to give the intellectual leadership demanded of him. The fortunate renewal of theology at the college and university level of the past decade is beginning to produce a theologically informed laity who expect of their parish priests more than average interest and competence in the whole range of ecclesiastical disciplines. Finally, the very fact of Vatican Council II has made it necessary for all priests, young and old, to "go back to school" if they are to communicate the insights of the Council to their people. There has never been a moment in the history of the Church when the obligation of intellectual excellence on the part of priests has been more grave: hence, the importance of a practical implementation of the directives (n. 19) of this Decree.

Heretofore, the work of clerical intellectual formation was thought to have been adequately discharged by the seminary course of studies leading to ordination. Now we realize more clearly that the work of formation has hardly begun. Nor is it enough to leave the rest to chance, with the hope that priests will take seriously their obligation to read and thus "keep up" on current trends in theology, scripture, liturgy and the like. All major industries and professions in our day, including the Armed Services, have carefully prepared programs of continuing education for their personnel. Promotion is conditioned to a large extent upon the use made of the means of ongoing formation. Furthermore, many Protestant Churches have long had serious programs of post-ordination education for their clergy. On the whole, the same cannot be said of the Catholic Church, even though steps in this direction have been taken in recent years in many parts of the United States and in other countries as well. One of the grave responsibilities of the national conferences of bishops will be to devise workable methods of providing continuing education for priests in the years to come.

The final point touched upon in the Decree is that of clerical remuneration. The problem is complex. So varied are the present economic conditions and histories and traditions of different parts of the Church that it was impossible for the Council to do more than offer some general guidelines. The principal teachings of the Decree are as follows:

1. Priests deserve an equitable remuneration so that they may live decently.

2. If no other means is provided, the faithful have an obligation to provide for the support of their clergy.

3. The salary of priests, account being taken of the nature of their office and of the conditions of

time and place, should be fundamentally the same for all in the same circumstances.

4. The salary received should be such that priests can fulfill their duty of charity and also have enough for a suitable annual vacation.

5. The so-called system of benefices (ecclesiastical offices to which a fixed revenue is attached) should be given up or at least reformed.

6. Some sort of social assistance, both for individual priests and for needy dioceses, should be established.

Both the letter and the spirit of the Decree suggest a radical rethinking of our present system of clerical remuneration, at least in many countries. As it is now, most diocesan priests receive an inadequate basic salary. They necessarily depend upon Mass stipends and other "stole fees" (the very title has an odious sound) to augment their income. Furthermore, the differences in the "net gain" from parish to parish within a diocese (and also from diocese to diocese within the same country or region) are sometimes shocking. In light of what the Council has said in this Decree and elsewhere about the collegial nature of the priestly collaborators of the bishop, such inequities should cease. Although the system of benefices strictly so-called does not exist in the United States, nonetheless the "appearance of merchandising" (to use the phrase in paragraph 17) is not always totally absent from the Church's most sacred spiritual functions. Surely some more straightforward and mature method of clerical support could be worked out which would effectively rid the Church, once and for all, of the "clink of money around the altar".

The ultimate concern of the Council is for the *spiritual freedom* of priests. The Decree does not plead for clerical wealth or a standard of living on the part of the clergy which is above that of their people. However, it does wish to provide for the material needs of priests that will permit them to live in decent comfort and be free from an anxious concern for the future. Thus they can "practice poverty with a readier appreciation of the Gospel and devote themselves completely to the salvation of souls".

CONCLUSION

The Decree has spoken much about the ideal of the priestly life. In fact, it offers a challenge to the ordained ministers of Christ that, given human weakness, may well be discouraging. In the final lines of the document, therefore, the fathers of the Council express their understanding of, and sympathy for, the concrete difficulties of the ministry and the loneliness and struggles that are experienced by so many priests today. The words of encouragement and of gratitude which conclude the *Decree on the Ministry and Life of Priests* are very much in order. Men in public positions are inevitably exposed to just and unjust criticism and attack. Their vices are seldom unknown or ignored for long, while their virtues and their fidelity are at times passed over in silence. Priests need to be assured of the affection in which they are held. Much is being demanded of them today. Although they have already given much, the Church is confident that they will give still more in the future.

Decretum

De Presbyterorum

Ministerio Et Vita

DECREE ON
THE MINISTRY AND
LIFE OF PRIESTS

Promulgated by Pope Paul VI
December 7, 1965

The *Decree on the Ministry and Life of Priests* was translated by Rev. Joseph Cunnane, C.C., D.D., and carefully checked by Very Rev. Michael Mooney, D.D. and Rev. Enda Lyons.

PAUL BISHOP

SERVANT OF THE SERVANTS OF GOD
TOGETHER WITH THE FATHERS OF THE SACRED COUNCIL
COMMITS TO PERMANENT RECORD

DECREE ON
THE MINISTRY AND
LIFE OF PRIESTS

INTRODUCTION

1. This sacred Council has already on several occasions drawn the attention of the world to the excellence of the order of priesthood in the Church.[1] However, since a most important and increasingly difficult role is being assigned to this order in the renewal of Christ's Church, it has been thought that it would be extremely useful to treat of the priesthood at greater length and depth. What is said here applies to all priests. It refers in a special way to those who are engaged in the care of souls. It is to be applied to regular clergy insofar as its provisions suit their circumstances.

Through the sacred ordination and mission

---

[1] *Constitution on the Sacred Liturgy,* Dec. 4, 1963: *A.A.S.* 56 (1964), pp. 97ff.; *Dogmatic Constitution on the Church,* Nov. 21, 1964: *A.A.S.* 57 (1965), pp. 5ff.; *Decree on the Pastoral Office of Bishops in the Church,* Oct. 28, 1965; *Decree on Priestly Training,* Oct. 28, 1965.

that they receive from the bishops, priests are promoted to the service of Christ, the teacher, priest and king; they are given a share in his ministry, through which the Church is here on earth being ceaselessly built up into the People of God, Christ's body and the temple of the Spirit. For that reason the Council has issued the following Decree with the aim of giving more effective support to the ministry of priests and making better provision for their life in the often vastly changed circumstances of the pastoral and human scene.

CHAPTER I
The Priesthood in the Church's Mission

Nature of the Priesthood

2. The Lord Jesus "whom the Father has made holy and sent into the world" (John 10, 36) makes his whole mystical body share in the anointing of the Spirit wherewith he has been anointed:[1] for in that body all the faithful are made a holy and kingly priesthood. They offer spiritual sacrifices to God through Jesus Christ and they proclaim the virtues of him who has called them out of darkness into his admirable light.[2] Therefore, there is no such thing as a member that has not a share in the mission of the whole body. Rather, every single member ought to sanctify Jesus in his heart[3] and by the spirit of prophecy give testimony of Jesus.[4]

However, the Lord also appointed certain

---

[1] Cf. Matt. 3, 16; Luke 4, 18; Acts 4, 27; 10, 38.

[2] Cf. 1 Pet. 2, 5. 9.

[3] Cf. 1 Pet. 3, 15.

[4] Cf. Apoc. 19, 10; *Dogmatic Constitution on the Church,* Nov. 21, 1964, n. 35: *A.A.S.* 57 (1965), pp. 40-1.

men as ministers in order that they might be united in one body in which "all the members have not the same function" (Rom. 12, 4). These men were to hold in the community of the faithful the sacred power of order, that of offering sacrifice and forgiving sins,[5] and they were to exercise the priestly office publicly on behalf of men in the name of Christ. Thus, Christ sent the apostles as he himself had been sent by the Father,[6] and then through the apostles he made their successors, the bishops,[7] sharers in his consecration and mission. The function of the bishops' ministry was handed over in a subordinate degree to priests[8] so that they might be appointed in the order of the priesthood and be co-workers of the episcopal order[9] for the proper fulfillment of the apostolic mission that had been entrusted to it by Christ.

Because it is joined with the episcopal order, the office of priests shares in the authority by which Christ himself builds up and sanctifies and rules his body. Hence the priesthood of priests, while presupposing the sacraments of initiation, is nevertheless conferred by its own particular sacrament. Through that sacrament priests are signed by the anointing of the Holy Spirit with a special character

---

[5] Council of Trent, Sess. XXIII, ch. 1, can. 1: Denz. 957, 961 (1764, 1771).

[6] Cf. John 20, 21; *Dogmatic Constitution on the Church,* Nov. 21, 1964, n. 18: *A.A.S.* 57 (1965), pp. 21-2.

[7] Cf. *Dogmatic Constitution on the Church,* Nov. 21, 1964, n. 28: *A.A.S.* 57 (1965), pp. 33-6.

[8] *Ibid.*

[9] Cf. Preface, "Ordination of a Priest," in the *Roman Pontifical.* These words are also found in the *Sacramentary of Verona* (ed. L. C. Möhlberg: Rome, 1956), p. 122; in the *Missale Francorum* (ed. L. C. Möhlberg: Rome, 1957), p. 9; in the *Liber Sacramentorum Romanae Ecclesiae* (ed. L. C. Möhlberg: Rome, 1960), p. 25; in the *Pontificale Romanum-Germanicum* (ed. Vogel-Elze: Vatican City, 1963), Vol. I, p. 34.

and so are configured to Christ the priest in such a way that they are able to act in the person of Christ the head.[10]

Since they share in the function of the apostles in their own degree, priests are given the grace by God to be the ministers of Jesus Christ among the nations, fulfilling the sacred task of the Gospel, that the oblation of the Gentiles may be made acceptable and sanctified in the Holy Spirit.[11] It is by the apostolic herald of the Gospel that the People of God is called together and gathered so that all who belong to this People, sanctified as they are by the Holy Spirit, may offer themselves "as a sacrifice, living, holy, pleasing to God" (Rom. 12, 1). Through the ministry of priests the spiritual sacrifice of the faithful is completed in union with the sacrifice of Christ, the only mediator, which in the eucharist is offered through the priests' hands in the name of the whole Church in an unbloody and sacramental manner until the Lord himself comes.[12] The ministry of priests is directed to this and finds its consummation in it. For their ministration, which begins with the announcement of the Gospel, draws its force and power from the sacrifice of Christ and tends to this end, that "the whole redeemed city—that is, the whole assembly and community of the saints—should be offered as a universal sacrifice to God through the high priest who offered himself in his passion for us that we might be the body of so great a head".[13]

Therefore, the object for which priests strive by their ministry and life is the procuring of the glory

---

[10] Cf. *Dogmatic Constitution on the Church*, Nov. 21, 1964, n. 10: *A.A.S.* 57 (1965), pp. 14-5.

[11] Cf. Rom. 15, 16 (Greek).

[12] Cf. 1 Cor. 11, 26.

[13] St. Augustine, *De civitate Dei*, 10, 6: *P.L.* 41, 284.

of God the Father in Christ. That glory consists in men's conscious, free and grateful acceptance of God's plan as completed in Christ and their manifestation of it in their whole life. Thus, whether they devote themselves to prayer and adoration, or preach the Word, or offer the eucharistic sacrifice and administer the other sacraments, or exercise other services for the benefit of men, priests contribute at the same time to the increase of God's glory and men's growth in the divine life. And all these activities, since they flow from the pasch of Christ, will find their consummation in the glorious coming of the same Lord when he shall have delivered up the kingdom to God and the Father.[14]

Place of Priests in the World

3. While being taken from among men and appointed for men in the things that pertain to God so that they may offer gifts and sacrifices for sins,[15] priests live with the rest of men as with brothers. So also the Lord Jesus, the Son of God, a man sent by the Father to men, dwelt among us and willed to be made like to his brothers in all things save only sin.[16] The apostles in their turn imitated him, and St. Paul, the teacher of the Gentiles, the man "set apart for the Gospel of God" (Rom. 1, 1), declared that he became all things to all men that he might save all.[17]

The priests of the New Testament are, by their vocation and ordination, set apart in some way in the midst of the People of God, but this is

---

14 Cf. 1 Cor. 15, 24.
15 Cf. Heb. 5, 1.
16 Cf. Heb. 2, 17; 4, 15.
17 Cf. 1 Cor. 9, 19-23 (Vulgate).

not in order that they should be separated from
that People or from any man, but rather that they
should be completely consecrated to the task for
which God chooses them.[18] They could not be the
servants of Christ unless they were witnesses and
dispensers of a life other than that of this earth.
On the other hand, they would be powerless to
serve men if they remained aloof from their life
and circumstances.[19] Their very ministry makes a

[18] Cf. Acts 13, 2.

[19] "Such anxiety for religious and moral perfection is more
and more demanded even by the external conditions in which
the Church lives out her life, for she cannot remain immov-
able and indifferent to the changes in the human scene around
her which in many ways influence her policy and impose limits
and conditions upon her. It is quite clear that the Church is
not isolated from the human community, but is situated in it,
and hence that her children are influenced and guided by it,
that they imbibe its culture, obey its laws and adopt its customs. Now this intercourse of the Church with human society
constantly gives rise to difficult problems. These are particularly serious at present. . . . The Apostle of the Gentiles
addressed this exhortation to the Christians of his time: 'Do
not bear the yoke with unbelievers. For what has justice in
common with inequity? Or what fellowship has light with
darkness? . . . Or what part has the believer with the unbe-
liever?' (2 Cor. 6, 14-15). For this reason those who presently
hold the position of educators and teachers in the Church
must impress upon Catholic youth their outstanding dignity
and the duty, arising from this, of living in this world but not
according to the sentiments of this world. This will be in conformity with the prayer made by Christ for his disciples: 'I
do not pray that thou take them out of the world, but that
thou keep them from evil. They are not of the world, even as
I am not of the world' (John 17, 15-16). The Church adopts
this prayer as her own.

"At the same time, however, such a difference as this does
not mean the same thing as separation. It does not profess
neglect or fear or contempt. For when the Church makes a
distinction between herself and the human race, so far is she
from setting herself in opposition to it that she rather is
joined with it" (Paul VI, Encyclical Letter *Ecclesiam suam*,
Aug 6, 1964: *A.A.S.* 56 [1964], pp. 627, 638).

special claim on them not to conform themselves to this world.[20] Nevertheless, it requires at the same time that they should live among men in this world and that as good shepherds they should know their sheep and should also seek to lead back those who do not belong to this fold, so that they too may hear the voice of Christ and that there may be one fold and one shepherd.[21]

In the pursuit of this aim priests will be helped by cultivating those virtues that are rightly held in high esteem in human relations. Such qualities are goodness of heart, sincerity, strength and constancy of mind, careful attention to justice, courtesy and others which the apostle Paul recommends when he says: "Whatever things are true, whatever honorable, whatever just, whatever holy, whatever lovable, whatever of good repute, if there be any virtue, if anything worthy of praise, think upon these things" (Phil. 4, 8).[22]

---

20 Cf. Rom. 12, 2.

21 Cf. John 10, 14-16.

22 Cf. St. Polycarp, *Epist. ad Philippenses* VI, 1: "Let priests also be disposed to pity, merciful to all, leading back the erring, visiting all the sick, not neglecting the widow, the orphan or the poor. Rather let them be always solicitous for good in the sight of God and men, refraining from all anger, acceptance of persons and unjust judgment, completely avoiding all avarice, slow to believe evil about anyone. Let them not be oversevere in judgment, knowing that we are all debtors of sin" (ed. F. X. Funk, *Patres Apostolici* I, p. 303).

CHAPTER II
The Ministry of Priests

I Functions of Priests

Priests as Ministers of God's Word

4. The People of God is formed into one in the first place by the Word of the living God,[1] which is quite rightly sought from the mouth of priests.[2] Since no one can be saved who has not first believed,[3] it is the first task of priests, as co-workers of the bishops, to preach the Gospel of God to all men.[4] In this way they carry out the Lord's command: "Go into the whole world and preach the Gospel to every creature" (Mark 16, 15),[5] and thus set up and increase the People of

---

[1] Cf. 1 Pet. 1, 23; Acts 6, 7; 12, 24. "They [the apostles] preached the Word of truth and produced churches" (St. Augustine, *In Ps.*, 44, 23: *P.L.* 36, 508).

[2] Cf. Mal. 2, 7; 1 Tim. 4, 11-13; 2 Tim. 4, 5; Tit. 1, 9.

[3] Cf. Mark 16, 16.

[4] Cf. 2 Cor. 11, 7. What is said of bishops holds also for priests, since they are the co-workers of the bishops. Cf. *Statuta Ecclesiae Antiqua,* ch. 3 (ed. Ch. Munier: Paris, 1960), p. 79; *Decretum Gratiani* I, C. 6, D. 88 (ed. Friedberg), p. 307; Council of Trent, *De reform.*, Sess. V, ch. 2, n. 9 *(Conc. Oec. Decreta,* ed. Herder: Rome, 1963, p. 645); Sess XXIV, ch. 4, p. 739; *Dogmatic Constitution on the Church,* Nov. 21, 1964: *A.A.S.* 57 (1965), pp. 29-31.

[5] Cf. *Constitutiones Apostolorum* II, 26, 7: "Let [priests] be the teachers of divine knowledge, since the Lord himself also commanded us, saying: 'Go, therefore, and teach. . . .'" (ed. F. X. Funk, *Didascalia et Constitutiones Apostolorum* I [Paderborn, 1905], p. 105); *Leonine Sacramentary* and other sacramentaries, including the Preface, "Ordination of a Priest," in the *Roman Pontifical:* "By this providence, O Lord, you have added teachers of the faith to the apostles of your Son, and

God. For by the saving Word of God faith is aroused in the heart of unbelievers and nourished in the heart of believers. By this faith, then, the congregation of the faithful begins and grows, according to the saying of the Apostle: "Faith then depends on hearing, and hearing on the Word of Christ" (Rom. 10, 17).

Priests thus owe it to everyone to share with them the truth of the Gospel[6] in which they rejoice in the Lord. Therefore, whether by behaving themselves "honorably among the pagans" they lead people to glorify God,[7] or by openly preaching proclaim the mystery of Christ to unbelievers, or teach the Christian message or explain the Church's doctrine, or endeavor to treat of contemporary problems in the light of Christ's teaching—in every case their role is to teach not their own wisdom but the Word of God and to issue an urgent invitation to all men to conversion and to holiness.[8] Moreover, the priest's preaching, often very difficult in present-day conditions, if it is to become more effective in moving the minds of his hearers, must expound the Word of God not merely in a general and abstract way but by an application of the eternal truth of the Gospel to the concrete circumstances of life.

---

through them they filled the whole earth with preachers (or: preachings) of the second rank"; "Preface for the Ordination of a Priest" in the *Book of Orders of the Mozarabic Liturgy:* "The teacher of peoples and the ruler of subjects, let him keep the Catholic faith in well-ordained fashion and announce true salvation to all" (ed. M. Férotin: Paris, 1904, col. 55).

[6] Cf. Gal. 2, 5.

[7] Cf. 1 Pet. 2, 12.

[8] Cf. the rite of ordination of a priest in the Alexandrian Church of the Jacobites: "Gather your people to the word of doctrine like a nurse who cherishes her children" (H. Denzinger, *Ritus Orientalium,* vol. II [Würzburg, 1863], p. 14).

Thus, the ministry of the Word is exercised in many different ways according to the needs of the hearers and the spiritual gifts of preachers. In non-Christian territories or societies people are led by the proclamation of the Gospel to faith and the saving sacraments.[9] In the Christian community itself, on the other hand, especially for those who seem to have little understanding or belief underlying their practice, the preaching of the Word is required for the sacramental ministry itself, since the sacraments are sacraments of faith drawing their origin and nourishment from the Word.[10] This is of paramount importance in the case of the liturgy of the Word within the celebration of Mass where there is an inseparable union of the proclamation of the Lord's death and resurrection, the response of its hearers and the offering itself by which Christ confirmed the new covenant in his blood. In this offering the faithful share both by their sacrificial sentiments and by the reception of the sacrament.[11]

---

[9] Cf. Matt. 28, 19; Mark 16, 16; Tertullian, *De baptismo*, 14, 2 (*Corpus Christianorum*, Series latina, I, p. 289, nn. 11-13); St. Athanasius, *Adv. Arianos*, 2, 42 (*P.G.* 26, 237); St. Jerome, *In Mat.*, 28, 19 (*P.L.* 26, 218b-c): "First they teach all the nations; then they baptize with water those who have been taught. For it cannot be that the body should receive the sacrament of baptism unless the soul has previously received the truth of the faith"; St. Thomas, *Expositio primae Decretalis*, n. 1: "When our Savior was sending his disciples to preach, he gave them three injunctions. First, that they should teach the faith; second, that they should initiate believers through the sacraments. . . ." (ed. Marietti, *Opuscula Theologica* [Turin-Rome, 1954], n. 1138).

[10] Cf. *Constitution on the Sacred Liturgy*, Dec. 4, 1963, n. 35: *A.A.S.* 56 (1964), p. 109.

[11] Cf. *ibid.*, nn. 33, 35, 48, 52 (pp. 108-109, 113, 114).

Priests as Ministers of the Sacraments and the Eucharist

5. God, who alone is the holy one and sanctifier, has willed to take men as allies and helpers who would become humble servants in his work of sanctification. The purpose, then, for which priests are consecrated by God through the ministry of the bishop is that they should be made sharers in a special way in Christ's priesthood and, by carrying out sacred functions, act as the ministers of him who through his Spirit continually exercises his priestly function for our benefit in the liturgy.[12] By baptism priests introduce men into the People of God; by the sacrament of penance they reconcile sinners with God and the Church; by the anointing of the sick they relieve those who are ill; and especially by the celebration of Mass they offer Christ's sacrifice sacramentally. As St. Ignatius the Martyr already asserted in the early Church,[13] in the celebration of all the sacraments priests are hierarchically united with the bishop in various ways and so make him present in a certain sense in individual assemblies of the faithful.[14]

But the other sacraments, and indeed all ecclesiastical ministries and works of the apostolate, are bound up with the eucharist and are directed toward it.[15] For in the most blessed eucharist is con-

---

[12] Cf. *ibid.*, n. 7, pp. 100-1; Pius XII, Encyclical Letter *Mystici corporis*, June 29, 1943: *A.A.S.* 35 (1943), p. 230.

[13] St. Ignatius Martyr, *Smyrn.*, 8, 1-2 (ed. F. X. Funk, p. 282, nn. 6-15); *Constitutiones Apostolorum* VIII, 12, 3 (ed. F. X. Funk, p. 496); VIII, 29, 2 (p. 532).

[14] Cf. *Dogmatic Constitution on the Church*, Nov. 21, 1964, n. 28: *A.A.S.* 57 (1965), pp. 33-6.

[15] "The Eucharist is, as it were, the completion of the spiritual life and the end of all the sacraments" (St. Thomas, *Summa Theol.* III, q. 73, a. 3 c); cf. *Summa Theol.* III, q. 65, a. 3.

tained the whole spiritual good of the Church,[16] namely, Christ himself, our pasch, and the living bread that gives life to men through his flesh— that flesh which is given life and gives life through the Holy Spirit. Thus, men are invited and led to offer themselves, their works and all creation with Christ. For this reason, the eucharist appears as the source and the summit of all preaching of the Gospel: catechumens are gradually led to participation in the eucharist, while the faithful who have already been consecrated in baptism and confirmation are fully incorporated in the body of Christ by the reception of the eucharist.

Therefore, the eucharistic celebration is the center of the assembly of the faithful over which the priest presides. Hence, priests teach the faithful to offer the divine Victim to God the Father in the sacrifice of the Mass and, with the victim, to make an offering of their whole life. In the spirit of Christ the pastor, they instruct them to submit their sins to the Church with a contrite heart in the sacrament of penance so that daily they may be more and more converted to the Lord, remembering his words: "Repent, for the kingdom of heaven is at hand" (Matt. 4, 17). They teach them to take part in the celebrations of the sacred liturgy in such a way as to also achieve sincere prayer in them. They guide them to the exercise of an ever more perfect spirit of prayer throughout their lives in proportion to each one's graces and needs. They lead all the faithful on to the observance of the duties of their particular state in life, and those who are more advanced, to the carrying out of the evangelical counsels in the way suited to their individual cases. Finally, they train the faithful so that they will be

---

[16] Cf. St. Thomas, *Summa Theol.* III, q. 65, a. 3, ad 1; q. 79, a. 1 c and ad 1.

able to sing in their hearts to the Lord with psalms and hymns and spiritual canticles, giving thanks always for all things in the name of our Lord Jesus Christ to God the Father.[17]

By their fulfillment of the divine office, priests themselves should extend to the different hours of the day the praise and thanksgiving they offer in the celebration of the eucharist. Through the office, they pray to God in the name of the Church for the whole people entrusted to them and in fact for the whole world.

The house of prayer, in which the most holy eucharist is celebrated and reserved, where the faithful assemble, and where is worshiped the presence of the Son of God our Savior, offered for us on the sacrificial altar for the help and consolation of the faithful—this house ought to be in good taste and a worthy place for prayer and sacred ceremonial.[18] In it pastors and the faithful are called upon to respond with grateful hearts to the gifts of him who through his humanity is unceasingly pouring the divine life into the members of his body.[19] Priests ought to go to the trouble of prop-

---

[17] Cf. Eph. 5, 19-20.

[18] Cf. St. Jerome, *Epist.*, 114, 2: ". . . consecrated chalices and sacred vestments and the other things that have to do with the worship of the Lord's passion . . . because of their association with the body and blood of the Lord, are to be venerated with the same reverence as his body and blood" (*P.L.* 22, 934); also cf. *Constitution on the Sacred Liturgy*, Dec. 4, 1963, nn. 122-127: *A.A.S.* 56 (1964), pp. 130-2.

[19] Moreover, let them not omit to make each day a visit to the most blessed sacrament, which is to be reserved in the most noble place and in the most honorable way possible in churches according to liturgical laws, since this visit will be at once a proof of gratitude, a pledge of love and an act of adoration due to Christ present in this same sacrament" (Paul VI, Encyclical Letter *Mysterium fidei*, Sept. 3, 1965: *A.A.S.* 57 (1965), p. 771.

erly cultivating liturgical knowledge and art so that, by means of their liturgical ministry, God the Father, Son and Holy Spirit may daily be more perfectly praised by the Christian communities entrusted to their care.

Priests as Rulers of God's People

6. Priests exercise the function of Christ as pastor and head in proportion to their share of authority. In the name of the bishop they gather the family of God as a brotherhood endowed with the spirit of unity and lead it in Christ through the Spirit to God the Father.[20] For the exercise of this ministry, as for the rest of the priest's functions, a spiritual power is given them, a power whose purpose is to build up.[21] And in building up the Church priests ought to treat everyone with the greatest kindness after the model of our Lord. They should act toward people not according to what may please men,[22] but according to the demands of Christian doctrine and life. They should teach them and warn them as their dearest children,[23] according to the words of the Apostle: "Be urgent in season, out of season; reprove, entreat, rebuke with all patience and teaching" (2 Tim. 4, 2).[24]

For this reason, it is the priests' part as instructors of the people in the faith to see to it, either personally or through others, that each mem-

---

[20] Cf. *Dogmatic Constitution on the Church,* Nov. 21, 1964, n. 28: *A.A.S.* 57 (1965), pp. 33-6.

[21] Cf. 2 Cor. 10, 8; 13, 10.

[22] Cf. Gal. 1, 10.

[23] Cf. 1 Cor. 4, 14.

[24] Cf. *Didascalia* II, 34, 3; II, 46, 6; II, 47, 1; *Constitutiones Apostolorum* II, 47, 1 (ed. F. X. Funk, *Didascalia et Constitutiones* I, pp. 116, 142-143).

ber of the faithful shall be led in the Holy Spirit to the full development of his own vocation in accordance with the Gospel teaching, and to sincere and active charity and to that freedom with which Christ has made us free.[25] Very little good will be achieved by ceremonies however beautiful or societies however flourishing if they are not directed toward educating people to reach Christian maturity.[26] To encourage this maturity priests should make their help available to people to enable them to determine the solution to their problems and God's will in the great or small crises of life.

Christians must also be trained so as not to live only for themselves. Rather, according to the demands of the new law of charity, every man as he has received grace ought to minister it one to another,[27] and in this way all should carry out their duties in a Christian way in the community of their fellowmen.

Although priests owe service to everyone, the poor and the weaker ones have been committed to their care in a special way. It was with these that the Lord himself associated,[28] and the preaching of the Gospel to them is given as a sign of his messianic mission.[29] With special diligence, priests should also seek out youth. This applies also to married couples and parents. It is desirable that these should meet in friendly groups to help each other in the task of more easily and more fully living in a Christian way a life that is often dif-

---

25 Cf. Gal. 4, 3; 5, 1. 13.

26 Cf. St. Jerome, *Epist.*, 58, 7: "What use is it that walls glitter with gems while Christ dies in the person of a poor man?" (*P.L.* 22, 584).

27 Cf. 1 Pet. 4, 10ff.

28 Cf. Matt. 25, 34-45.

29 Cf. Luke 4, 18.

ficult. Priests should keep in mind that all religious, men and women, being a particularly eminent group in the Lord's house, are deserving of having special care directed to their spiritual progress for the good of the whole Church. Finally, priests ought to be especially devoted to the sick and the dying, visiting them and comforting them in the Lord.[30]

The pastor's task is not limited to individual care of the faithful. It extends by right also to the formation of a genuine Christian community. But if a community spirit is to be properly cultivated, it must embrace not only the local Church but the universal Church. A local community ought not merely to promote the care of the faithful within itself but should be imbued with the missionary spirit and smooth the path to Christ for all men. Moreover, it must regard as its special charge those under instruction and the newly converted who are to be gradually educated in knowing and living the Christian life.

However, no Christian community is built up which does not grow from, and hinge on, the celebration of the most holy eucharist. From this all education for community spirit must begin.[31] This

---

[30] Other classes can be mentioned: e.g., migrants, itinerants, etc. These are dealt with in the *Decree on the Pastoral Office of Bishops in the Church* (Oct. 28, 1965).

[31] Cf. *Didascalia* II, 59, 1-3: "In your teaching, order and exhort the people to visit the church and never to be entirely absent, but to assemble always, and not impoverish the church by staying away and making the body of Christ less a member. . . . Therefore, since you are members of Christ, do not separate yourselves from the Church by failing to be united; having Christ, your head, present and communicating with you according to his promise, do not neglect yourselves or alienate the Savior from his members or disperse his body. . . ." (ed. F. X. Funk, I, p. 170) ; Paul VI, Allocution *To the*

eucharistic celebration, to be full and sincere, ought to lead, on the one hand, to the various works of charity and mutual help, and, on the other hand, to missionary activity and the various forms of Christian witness.

In addition, the ecclesial community exercises a truly motherly function in leading souls to Christ by its charity, its prayer, its example and its penitential works. For it constitutes an effective instrument for showing or smoothing the path toward Christ and his Church for those who have not yet found faith, while encouraging, supporting and strengthening believers also for their spiritual struggles.

In building up a community of Christians, priests can never be the servants of any human ideology or party. Rather, their task as heralds of the Gospel and pastors of the Church is the attainment of the spiritual growth of the body of Christ.

II Priests' Relations with Others
Relation between Bishops and the Priestly Body

7. All priests share with the bishops the one identical priesthood and ministry of Christ. Consequently, the very unity of their consecration and mission requires their hierarchical union with the order of bishops.[32] This unity is best shown on some occasions by liturgical concelebration, and priests also affirm their union with the bishops in the eucharistic celebration.[33] Because of the gift of the

---

Italian Clergy at the 13th "Week of Pastoral Renewal", delivered at Orvieto, Sept. 6, 1963: *A.A.S.* 55 (1963), pp. 750ff.

[32] Cf. *Dogmatic Constitution on the Church*, Nov. 21, 1964, n. 28: *A.A.S.* 57 (1965), p. 35.

[33] Cf. the so-called *Ecclesiastical Constitution of the Apostles*, XVIII: "Priests are fellow-participants in the mysteries and fellow-soldiers of the bishops" (ed. Th. Schermann, *Die allgemeine Kirchenordnung* I [Paderborn, 1914], p.

Holy Spirit that has been given to priests at their ordination, bishops, therefore, should regard them as their indispensable helpers and advisors in the ministry and in the task of teaching, sanctifying and shepherding the People of God.[34] This has been forcefully emphasized from the earliest ages of the Church by the liturgical documents. These solemnly pray to God for the pouring out upon the priest to be ordained of "the spirit of grace and counsel, that he may help and govern the people in a pure heart",[35] just as in the desert the spirit of Moses was made to grow into the minds of the seventy wise men[36] "whom he employed as helpers and easily governed countless multitudes among the people".[37]

26; A. Harnack, *T. u. U.*, II, 4, p. 13, nn. 18-19); Pseudo-Jerome, *De Septem Ordinibus Ecclesiae*: ". . . in the blessing, they are sharers in the mysteries with the bishops" (ed. A. W. Kalff [Würzburg, 1937], p. 45) ; St. Isidore of Seville, *De Ecclesiasticis Officiis*, ch. VII: "They are set over the Church of God, and in the celebration of the eucharist they are the associates of the bishops, as they are also in teaching the people and in the office of preaching" (*P.L.* 83, 787) .

[34] Cf. *Didascalia* II, 28, 4 (ed. F. X. Funk, p. 108) ; *Constitutiones Apostolorum* II, 28, 4; II, 34, 3 (*ibid.*, pp. 109, 117).

[35] *Constitutiones Apostolorum* VIII, 16, 4 (ed. F. X. Funk, I, p. 522, n. 13) ; cf. *Epitome Constitutiones Apostolorum* VI (*ibid.*, II, p. 80, nn. 3-4); *Testamentum Domini*: ". . . give him the Spirit of grace, counsel and magnanimity, the spirit of the priesthood . . . to help and govern your people in work, in fear and in a pure heart" (tr. I. E. Rahmani [Mainz, 1899], p. 69; also in *Trad. Apost.* (ed. B. Botte, *La Tradition Apostolique* [Münster, 1963], p. 20) .

[36] Cf. Num. 11, 16-25.

[37] Cf. Preface for the ordination of a priest in the *Roman Pontifical*. These words are also contained in the Leonine, Gelasian and Gregorian sacramentaries. Similar expressions are found in the Eastern liturgies; cf. *Trad. Apost.*: ". . . look upon this your servant and impart to him the spirit of grace and counsel that he may aid the priests and rule your people with a clean heart, as you looked upon the people of your

On account of this common sharing in the same priesthood and ministry, bishops are to regard their priests as brothers and friends,[38] and they are to take the greatest possible interest in their welfare, both temporal and especially spiritual. For on their shoulders particularly falls the burden of sanctifying their priests;[39] therefore, they are to exercise the greatest care in the progressive formation of their diocesan body of priests.[40] They should be glad to listen to their priests' views and even consult them and hold conferences with them about matters that concern the needs of pastoral work and the good of the diocese. For this to be reduced to practice, however, a group or senate of priests[41]

---

choice and commanded Moses to choose elders whom you filled with your spirit which you have given to your servant" (from the ancient Latin version of Verona, ed. B. Botte, *La Tradition Apostolique de S. Hippolyte. Essai de reconstruction* [Münster, 1963], p. 20); *Constitutiones Apostolorum* VIII, 16, 4 (ed. F. X. Funk, I, p. 522, nn. 16-17); *Epit. Const. Apost.* VI (ed. F. X. Funk, II, p. 20, nn. 5-7) ; *Testamentum Domini* (tr. I. E. Rahmani [Mainz, 1899], p. 69) ; *Euchologium Serapionis* XXVII (ed. F. X. Funk, *Didascalia et Constitutiones* II, p. 190, nn. 1-7) ; *Ritus Ordinationis in ritu Maronitarum* (tr. H. Denzinger, *Ritus Orientalium* II [Würzburg, 1863], p. 161). Among the Fathers can be cited Theodore of Mopsuestia, *In 1 Tim.* 3, 8 (ed. Swete, II, pp. 119-21), and Theodore, *Quaestiones in Numeros* XVIII (P. G. 80, 372b).

38 Cf. *Dogmatic Constitution on the Church*, Nov. 21, 1964, n. 28: *A.A.S.* 57 (1965), p. 35.

39 Cf. John XXIII, Encyclical Letter *Sacerdotii nostri primordia*, Aug. 1, 1959: *A.A.S.* 51 (1959), p. 576; St. Pius X, Exhortation to the Clergy *Haerent animo*, Aug. 4, 1908: *S. Pii X Acta*, vol. IV (1908), pp. 237ff.

40 Cf. *Decree on the Pastoral Office of Bishops in the Church*, Oct. 28, 1965, nn. 15-16.

41 In established law the Cathedral Chapter is regarded as the bishop's "senate and council" (*C.I.C.*, can. 391) or, in its absence, the group of diocesan consultors (cf. *C.I.C.*, canons 423-8). However, it is desirable to reform these institutions in such a way as to make better provision for present-day

should be set up in a way suited to present-day needs,[42] and in a form and with rules to be determined by law. This group would represent the body of priests and by their advice could effectively help the bishop in the management of the diocese.

Priests for their part should keep in mind the fullness of the sacrament of orders that bishops enjoy and should reverence in their persons the authority of Christ the supreme pastor. They should therefore be attached to their bishop with sincere charity and obedience.[43] That priestly obedience, inspired through and through by the spirit of cooperation, is based on that sharing of the episcopal

---

needs. Clearly this group of priests differs from the pastoral council spoken of in the *Decree on the Pastoral Office of Bishops in the Church* (Oct. 28, 1965, n. 27) which includes laymen and whose function is confined to investigating questions of pastoral activity. On the question of priests as counselors of bishops, see *Didascalia* II, 28, 4 (ed. F. X. Funk, I, p. 108) ; also cf. *Const. Apost.* II, 28, 4 (ed. F. X. Funk, I, p. 109) ; St. Ignatius Martyr, *Magn.*, 6, 1 (ed. F. X. Funk, p. 234, nn. 10-16); *Trall.*, 3, 1 (ed. F. X. Funk, p. 244, nn. 10-12); Origen, *Adv. Celsum*, 3, 30: "Priests are counselors or *bouleutai*" (*P.G.* 11, 957d-960a).

[42] St. Ignatius Martyr, *Magn.*, 6, 1: "I exhort you to strive to do all things in the peace of God, the bishop presiding in the place of God and the priests in the place of the senate of apostles and the deacons who are so dear to me, having entrusted to them the ministry of Jesus Christ who was with the Father before all ages and finally appeared" (ed. F. X. Funk, p. 234, nn. 10-13) ; *idem, Trall.*, 3, 1: "Likewise let all reverence the deacons as Jesus Christ, and also the bishop who is the image of the Father, and the priests as the senate of God and the council of the apostles: without these one cannot speak of a Church" (*ibid.*, p. 244, nn. 10-12) ; St. Jerome, *In Isaiam*, II, 3 (*P.L.* 24, 61a): "We also have in the Church our senate, the group of priests."

[43] Cf. Paul VI, Allocution *To the Parish Priests and Lenten Preachers of Rome,* delivered in the Sistine Chapel, March 1, 1965: *A.A.S.* 57 (1965) , p. 326.

ministry which is conferred on priests by the sacrament of orders and the canonical mission.[44]

There is all the more need in our day for the union of priests with bishops because in our present age apostolic enterprises must necessarily take on many different forms for various reasons. In addition, they must often overstep the bounds of one parish or diocese. Therefore, no priest is sufficiently equipped to carry out his own mission alone and, as it were, single-handedly. He can only do so by joining forces with other priests, under the leadership of those who are the rulers of the Church.

Brotherly Bond and Cooperation between Priests

8. All priests who are constituted in the order of priesthood by the sacrament of orders are bound together by an intimate sacramental brotherhood; but in a special way they form one priestly body in the diocese to which they are attached under their own bishop, for even though they may be assigned different duties, yet they fulfill the one priestly service for people. Indeed, all priests are sent to cooperate in the same work. This is true whether the ministry they exercise be parochial or supraparochial, whether their task be research or teaching, or even if they engage in manual labor and share the lot of the workers—where that appears to be of advantage and has the approval of the competent authority—or, finally, if they carry out other

---

44 Cf. *Const. Apost.* VIII, 47, 39: "Priests . . . should do nothing without the decision of the bishop, for it is to him that the people of the Lord have been entrusted and from him an account of their souls will be demanded" (ed. F. X. Funk, p. 577).

apostolic works or those directed toward the apostolate. They all contribute to the same purpose, namely, the building up of the body of Christ, and this, especially in our times, demands many kinds of duties and fresh adaptations.

For this reason, it is of great importance that all priests, whether diocesan or regular, should help each other so that they may be fellow helpers of the truth.[45] Each is joined to the rest of the members of this priestly body by special ties of apostolic charity, of ministry and of brotherhood. This is signified liturgically from ancient times by the fact that the priests present at an ordination are invited to impose hands, along with the ordaining bishop, on the chosen candidate, and when priests concelebrate the sacred eucharist in a spirit of harmony. Therefore, priests are all united with their brother-priests by the bond of charity, prayer and total cooperation. In this way is shown forth that unity with which Christ willed his own to be perfected in one, so that the world might know that the Son had been sent by the Father.[46]

From this it follows that older priests should sincerely accept the younger ones as brothers and be a help to them in facing the first tasks and responsibilities of their ministry. They should also make an effort to understand their outlook, even though it may be different from their own, and they should give kindly encouragement to their projects. Young priests for their part are to respect the age and experience of their elders; they should consult with them on matters concerning the care of souls and willingly cooperate with them.

Under the influence of the spirit of brother-

---

45 Cf. 3 John 8.
46 Cf. John 17, 23.

hood priests should not forget hospitality,[47] and they should cultivate kindness and the sharing of goods.[48] They should be particularly concerned about those who are sick, the afflicted, the over-worked, the lonely, the exiled and the perse-cuted.[49] They should also be delighted to gather together for relaxation, remembering the words by which the Lord himself invited his weary apos-tles: "Come apart into a desert place and rest a while" (Mark 6, 31).

Moreover, in order to enable priests to find mutual help in cultivating the intellectual and spiritual life, to promote better cooperation among them in the ministry and to safeguard them from possible dangers arising from loneliness, it is nec-essary to foster some kind of community life or social relations among them. However, this can take different forms according to varying personal and pastoral needs: by priests' living together, where this is possible, or by their sharing a common table or at least meeting at frequent intervals. Associations of priests are also to be highly esteemed and diligently promoted, when, by means of rules recognized by the competent authority, they foster priestly holiness in the exercise of the ministry through a suitable and properly approved rule of life and through brotherly help, and thus aim at serving the whole order of priests.

Finally, because of the same brotherly bond of the priesthood, priests ought to realize that they have an obligation toward those who are laboring under difficulties. They should offer timely help to them, even by discreetly warning them where nec-

---

[47] Cf. Heb. 13, 1-2.
[48] Cf. Heb. 13, 16.
[49] Cf. Matt. 5, 10.

essary. They should always treat with fraternal charity and compassion those who have failed in certain ways. They should pray earnestly to God for them and never cease to show themselves to them as genuine brothers and friends.

Relation of Priests with Lay People

9. Even though the priests of the new law by reason of the sacrament of orders fulfill the preeminent and essential function of father and teacher among the People of God and on their behalf, they are, nevertheless, disciples of the Lord along with all the faithful and have been made partakers of the kingdom of God who has called them by his divine grace.[50] Priests, in common with all who have been reborn in the font of baptism, are brothers among brothers[51] as members of the same body of Christ which all are commanded to build up.[52]

Priests, therefore, should occupy their position of leadership as men who do not seek the things that are their own but the things that are Jesus Christ's.[53] They should unite their efforts with those of the lay faithful and conduct themselves among them after the example of the master who "has not come to be served but to serve, and to give his life as

[50] Cf. 1 Thess. 2, 12; Col. 1, 13.

[51] Cf. Matt. 23, 8; Paul VI, Encyclical Letter *Ecclesiam suam*, Aug. 6, 1964, n. 90: *A.A.S.* 58 (1964), p. 647; "From the very fact that we wish to be the pastors, fathers and teachers of men, it follows that we must act as their brothers."

[52] Cf. Eph. 4, 7. 16; *Const. Apost.* VIII, 1, 20: "The bishop moreover should not set himself up over the deacons or priests, nor the priests over the people, for the structure of the assembly is made up of members of both" (ed. F. X. Funk, I, p. 467).

[53] Cf. Phil. 2, 21.

a ransom for many" (Matt. 20, 28). Priests are to be sincere in their appreciation and promotion of the dignity of lay people and of the special role proper to the laity in the Church's mission. They should also have an unfailing respect for the just freedom that belongs to everyone in civil society. They should be willing to listen to lay people, give brotherly consideration to their wishes and recognize their experience and competence in different fields of human activity. In this way they will be able to recognize along with them the signs of the times.

While trying the spirits to see if they be of God,[54] they must discover with faith, recognize with joy and foster with diligence the many and varied charismatic gifts of the laity, whether these be of a humble or more exalted kind. Among the other gifts of God that are found abundantly among the faithful, special attention ought to be devoted to those graces by which a considerable number of people are attracted to greater heights of the spiritual life. Priests should also be confident in giving lay people charge of duties in the service of the Church, giving them freedom and opportunity for activity and even inviting them, when opportunity occurs, to take the initiative in undertaking projects of their own.[55]

Finally, priests have been placed in the midst of the laity so that they may lead them all to the unity of charity: "Love one another with fraternal charity, anticipating one another with honor" (Rom. 12, 10). Theirs is the task, then, of bringing about agreement between divergent outlooks in such a way that nobody may feel a stranger in the Christian

---

54 Cf. 1 John 4, 1.

55 Cf. *Dogmatic Constitution on the Church*, Nov. 21, 1964, n. 37: *A.A.S.* 57 (1965), pp. 42-3.

community. They are to be the defenders of the common good, for which they are responsible in the bishop's name, and at the same time the unwavering champions of truth lest the faithful be tossed about with every wind of doctrine.[56] Those who have abandoned the practice of the sacraments or even perhaps the faith are entrusted to priests as special objects of their care. They must not neglect to approach these as good shepherds.

Priests should keep in mind what has been laid down in regard to ecumenism[57] and not forget those fellow Christians who do not enjoy complete ecclesiastical union with us.

They will regard as committed to their charge all those who fail to recognize Christ as their Savior.

The faithful for their part ought to realize that they have obligations to their priests. They should treat them with filial love as being their fathers and pastors. They should also share their priests' anxieties and help them as far as possible by prayer and active work so that they may be better able to overcome difficulties and carry out their duties with greater success.[58]

III Distribution of Priests; Priestly Vocations

Proper Distribution of Priests

10. The spiritual gift received by priests in ordination does not merely prepare them for a limited and circumscribed mission, but for the

---

56 Cf. Eph. 4, 14.

57 Cf. *Decree on Ecumenism,* Nov. 21, 1964: *A.A.S.* 57 (1965) , pp. 90ff.

58 Cf. *Dogmatic Constitution on the Church,* Nov. 21, 1964, n. 37: *A.S.S.* 57 (1965) , pp. 42-3.

fullest—in fact, the universal—mission of salvation "even to the very ends of the earth" (Acts 1, 8), for every priestly ministry shares in the fullness of the mission entrusted by Christ to the apostles. The priesthood of Christ, of which priests have really been made sharers, is necessarily directed to all peoples and all times, and it is not confined by any bounds of blood, race or age, as was already typified in a mysterious way by the figure of Melchisedech.[59]

Priests should therefore recall that the solicitude of all the Churches ought to be their intimate concern. For this reason priests of those dioceses that are blessed with greater abundance of vocations should be prepared to offer themselves gladly—with the permission or encouragement of their own ordinary—for the exercise of their ministry in countries or missions or tasks that are hampered by a shortage of clergy.

In addition, the rules about incardination and excardination should be revised in such a way that, while this ancient institution remains intact, it will answer better to the pastoral needs of today. Where the nature of the apostolate demands this, not only the proper distribution of priests should be made easier but also the carrying out of special pastoral projects for the benefit of different social groups in any region or among any race in any part of the world. For this purpose there can be set up with advantage some international seminaries, special dioceses or personal prelacies and other such institutions to which—by methods to be decided for the individual undertaking and always without prejudice to the rights of local ordinaries—priests can be attached or incardinated for the common good of the whole Church.

---

[59] Cf. Heb. 7, 3.

As far as possible, however, priests are not to be sent alone into a new territory, especially if they are not yet well versed in its language and customs. Rather, after the example of Christ's disciples,[60] they should be sent at least in groups of two or three so that they may be of mutual help to one another. It is also advisable to pay careful attention to their spiritual life and their mental and bodily health. Where possible, places and conditions of work are to be prepared for them to suit each one's personal circumstances.

It will also be of the greatest advantage for those who go to a new territory to take the trouble to learn not only the language of the place but also the special psychological and social characteristics of the people they wish to serve in humility in order to establish the most perfect possible communication with them. In this way they will be following the example of St. Paul, who could say of himself: "For, free though I was as to all, unto all I have made myself a slave that I might gain the more converts. And I have become to the Jews a Jew that I might gain the Jews" (1 Cor. 9, 19-20).

Priests' Care for Priestly Vocations

11. The shepherd and bishop of our souls[61] set up his Church in such a way that the people whom he chose and acquired by his blood[62] would always and until the end of the world have their own priests, lest Christians be like sheep that have no shepherd.[63] The apostles realized this intention of Christ and, under the guidance of the Holy Spirit,

---

60 Cf. Luke 10, 1.
61 Cf. 1 Pet. 2, 25.
62 Cf. Acts 20, 28.
63 Cf. Matt. 9, 36.

considered it their duty to choose ministers who would "be competent in turn to teach others" (2 Tim. 2, 2). In fact, this duty belongs to the very nature of the priestly mission that causes the priest to share in the anxiety of the whole Church lest laborers should ever be wanting to the People of God here on earth.

However, since "a common interest exists . . . between the pilot of the ship and the passengers",[64] the whole Christian people ought to be made aware that it is their duty to cooperate in various ways, both by earnest prayer and by the other means available to them,[65] to ensure that the Church will always have those priests who are needed for the fulfillment of her divine mission. In the first place, then, priests are to make it their most cherished object to make clear to people the excellence and necessity of the priesthood. They do this by their preaching and by the personal witness of a life that shows clearly a spirit of service and a genuine paschal joy. Then they must spare no trouble or inconvenience in helping both youths and older men whom they prudently consider suitable for so great a ministry to prepare themselves properly so that they can be called at some time by the bishops, while preserving their full freedom, both external and internal. In the pursuit of this object, diligent and prudent spiritual direction is of the greatest advantage.

Parents, teachers and all who are in any way concerned in the education of boys and young men should train them in such a way that they will know the solicitude of the Lord for his flock and be alive to the needs of the Church. In this way they will be prepared, when the Lord calls, to answer

---

64 "Ordination of a Priest" in the *Roman Pontifical.*
65 Cf. *Decree on Priestly Training,* Oct. 28, 1965, n. 2.

generously with the prophet: "Here I am. . . .
Send me" (Is. 6, 8). However, it is emphatically
not to be expected that the voice of the Lord calling
should come to the future priest's ears in some ex-
traordinary way. Rather, it must be perceived and
judged through the signs by which God's will becomes known to prudent Christians in everyday life.
And these signs are to be studied attentively by
priests.[66]

Therefore, organizations for the promotion of
vocations, whether diocesan or national, are recommended highly to priests.[67] In sermons, in cate-
chetical instruction and in periodicals, the needs of
the local and universal Church are to be made
known clearly. The meaning and excellence of the
priestly ministry is to be highlighted—a ministry in
which the many trials are balanced by such great
joys, and especially one in which, as the Fathers
teach, the greatest witness of love can be given to
Christ.[68]

---

[66] "The voice of God which calls expresses itself in two
different ways that are marvelous and converging: one interior, that of grace, that of the Holy Spirit, that inexpressible
interior attraction which the silent and powerful voice of the
Lord exercises in the unfathomable depths of the human soul;
and the other one external, human, sensible, social, juridical,
concrete, that of the qualified minister of the Word of God,
that of the apostle, that of the hierarchy, an indispensable
instrument instituted and willed by Christ as a concrete means
of translating into the language of experience the message of
the Word and the divine precept. Such is the teaching of
Catholic doctrine with St. Paul: 'How are they to hear if no
one preaches? . . . Faith then depends on hearing' (Rom. 10,
14. 17)" (Paul VI, Allocution of May 5, 1965: *L'Osservatore
Romano,* May 6, 1965, p. 1) .

[67] Cf. *Decree on Priestly Training,* Oct. 28, 1965, n. 2.

[68] This is the teaching of the Fathers when they explain
Christ's words to Peter: "Dost thou love me? . . . Feed my
sheep" (John 21, 17). Cf. also St. John Chrysostom, *De
sacerdotio,* II, 1-2 (*P.G.* 47-48, 633); St. Gregory the Great,
Reg. Past. Liber, P. I. c. 5 (*P.L.* 77, 19a).

CHAPTER III
The Life of Priests

I Priests' Call to Perfection

Call of Priests to Holiness

12. By the sacrament of orders priests are configured to Christ the priest as servants of the head, so that, as co-workers with the episcopal order, they may build up the body of Christ, the Church. Like all Christians they have already received in the consecration of baptism the sign and gift of their great calling and grace. Thus they are enabled and obliged even in the midst of human weakness[1] to seek perfection, according to the Lord's word: "You therefore are to be perfect, even as your heavenly Father is perfect" (Matt. 5, 48).

However, priests are bound by a special reason to acquire this perfection. They are consecrated to God in a new way in their ordination and are made the living instruments of Christ the eternal priest and so are enabled to accomplish throughout all time that wonderful work of his which with supernatural efficacy restored the whole human race.[2] Therefore, since every priest in his own way assumes the person of Christ, he is endowed with a special grace. By this grace the priest, through serving the people committed to his care and all the People of God, is better able to pursue the perfection of Christ whose place he takes. The human weakness of his flesh is remedied by the holiness of him who became for us a high priest "holy, in-

[1] Cf. 2 Cor. 12, 9.
[2] Cf. Pius XI, Encyclical Letter *Ad catholici sacerdotii,* Dec. 20, 1935: *A.A.S.* 28 (1936), p. 10.

nocent, undefiled, set apart from sinners" (Heb. 7, 26).

Christ, whom the Father sanctified or consecrated and sent into the world,[3] "gave himself for us that he might redeem us from all iniquity and cleanse for himself an acceptable people, pursuing good works" (Tit. 2, 14), and in this way through his passion entered into his glory.[4] In a similar way, priests, who are consecrated by the anointing of the Holy Spirit and sent by Christ, mortify the works of the flesh in themselves and dedicate themselves completely to the service of people. Therefore, they are able, in the holiness with which they have been enriched in Christ, to make progress toward the perfect man.[5]

In this way they are made strong in the life of the spirit by exercising the ministration of the Spirit and of justice,[6] provided they are prepared to listen to the inspiration of the Spirit of Christ who gives them life and guidance. For it is through the sacred actions they perform every day, as through their whole ministry which they exercise in union with the bishop and their fellow priests, that they are set on the right course to perfection of life. The very holiness of priests is of the greatest benefit for the fruitful fulfillment of their ministry. While it is possible for God's grace to carry out the work of salvation through unworthy ministers, yet God ordinarily prefers to show his wonders through those men who are more submissive to the impulse and guidance of the Holy Spirit and who, because of their intimate union with Christ and their holi-

---

3 Cf. John 10, 36.
4 Cf. Luke 24, 26.
5 Cf. Eph. 4, 13.
6 Cf. 2 Cor. 3, 8-9.

ness of life, are able to say with St. Paul: "It is now no longer I that live, but Christ lives in me" (Gal. 2, 20).

For that reason this sacred Council, in the hope of attaining its pastoral objectives of interior renewal, of worldwide diffusion of the Gospel and of dialogue with the modern world, issues the strongest exhortation to all priests to strive always, by the use of all suitable means commended by the Church,[7] toward that greater holiness that will daily make them more effective instruments for the service of all God's people.

The Exercise of the Threefold Priestly Function Demands and Fosters Holiness

13. Priests will acquire holiness in their own distinctive way by exercising their functions sincerely and tirelessly in the Spirit of Christ. Since they are the ministers of the Word of God, they read and hear every day the Word of God that they must teach to others. If they strive at the same time to make it part of their own lives, they will become daily more perfect disciples of the Lord, according to the saying of the Apostle Paul to Timothy: "Meditate on these things; give thyself entirely to them, that thy progress may be manifest to all. Take heed to thyself and to thy teaching; be

---

7 Among others, cf. St. Pius X, Exhortation to the Clergy *Haerent animo*, Aug. 4, 1908: *S. Pii X Acta*, IV (1908), pp. 237ff.; Pius XI, Encyclical Letter *Ad catholici sacerdotii*, Dec. 20, 1935: *A.A.S.* 28 (1936), pp. 5ff.; Pius XII, Apostolic Exhortation *Menti nostrae*, Sept. 23, 1950: *A.A.S.* 42 (1950), pp. 657ff.; John XXIII, Encyclical Letter *Sacerdotii nostri primordia*, Aug. 1, 1959: *A.A.S.* 51 (1959), pp. 545ff.

earnest in them. For in so doing thou wilt save both thyself and those that hear thee" (1 Tim. 4, 15–16). For by seeking more effective ways of conveying to others what they have meditated,[8] they will savor more profoundly the "unfathomable riches of Christ" (Eph. 3, 8) and the many-sided wisdom of God.[9] By keeping in mind that it is the Lord who opens hearts[10] and that the excellence comes not from themselves but from the power of God,[11] they will be more intimately united with Christ the teacher and will be guided by his Spirit in the very act of teaching the Word. And by this close union with Christ they share in the charity of God, the mystery of which was kept hidden from all ages[12] to be revealed in Christ.

As ministers of the sacred mysteries, and especially in the sacrifice of the Mass, priests act in a special way in the person of Christ who gave himself as a victim to sanctify men. This is why they are invited to imitate what they handle so that, as they celebrate the mystery of the Lord's death, they may take care to mortify their members from evil habits and desires.[13]

In the mystery of the eucharistic sacrifice, in which priests fulfill their principal function, the work of our redemption is continually carried out.[14] For this reason the daily celebration of this sacrifice is earnestly recommended. This celebration is an act of Christ and the Church, even if it is impossible for

---

[8] Cf. St. Thomas, *Summa Theol.*, II-II, q. 188, a. 7.

[9] Cf. Heb. 3, 9-10.

[10] Cf. Acts 16, 14.

[11] Cf. 2 Cor. 4, 7.

[12] Cf. Eph. 3, 9.

[13] Cf. "Ordination of a Priest" in the *Roman Pontifical*.

[14] Cf. *Roman Missal,* "Prayer over the Gifts," 9th Sunday after Pentecost.

the faithful to be present.[15] Therefore, when priests unite themselves with the act of Christ the priest, they offer themselves completely to God each day, and by being nourished with Christ's body they share in the charity of him who gives himself as food to the faithful.

In the same way priests are united with the intention and the charity of Christ when they administer the sacraments. They do this in a special way by showing themselves to be always available to administer the sacrament of penance whenever it is reasonably requested by the faithful. In reciting the divine office they lend their voice to the Church who perseveres in prayer in the name of the whole human race, in union with Christ who "lives always to make intercession for them" (Heb. 7, 25).

While they govern and shepherd the People of God, priests are encouraged by the love of the good shepherd to give their lives for their sheep.[16] They also are prepared for the supreme sacrifice, following the example of those priests who even in our own times have not shrunk from laying down their lives. Since they are the instructors in the faith and are

---

15 "The Mass, even though it is celebrated privately, is still not private, but is the act of Christ and the Church. The Church, in the sacrifice which she offers, learns to offer herself as a universal sacrifice and applies the unique and infinite redemptive power of the sacrifice of the cross to the whole world for its salvation. For every Mass that is celebrated is offered not merely for the salvation of some souls but for that of the whole world. . . . Therefore, we recommend with paternal insistence to priests, who are our especial joy and our crown in the Lord, that . . . they celebrate Mass worthily and devoutly every day" (Paul VI, Encyclical Letter *Mysterium fidei*, Sept. 3, 1965, nn. 32-33: *A.A.S.* 57 (1965), pp. 761-2). Also cf. the *Constitution on the Sacred Liturgy*, Dec. 4, 1963, nn. 26-27: *A.A.S.* 56 (1964), p. 107.

16 Cf. John 10, 11.

themselves "free to enter the Holies in virtue of
the blood of Christ" (Heb. 10, 19), they approach
God "with a true heart in fullness of faith" (Heb.
10, 22). They set up a steadfast hope for their
faithful people[17] so that, by the exhortation wherewith God also exhorts them,[18] they may be able to
comfort those who are in great distress. As rulers
of the community they cultivate the form of asceticism suited to a pastor of souls, renouncing their
own convenience, seeking not what is to their own
advantage but what will benefit the many for salvation,[19] always making further progress toward a
more perfect fulfillment of their pastoral work,
and, where the need arises, prepared to break new
ground in pastoral methods under the guidance of
the Spirit of love who breathes where he wills.[20]

Unity and Harmony of the Life of Priests

14. In today's world, with so many duties that
people must undertake and the great variety of
problems vexing them and very often demanding
a speedy solution, there is often danger for those
whose energies are divided by different activities.
Priests who are perplexed and distracted by the
very many obligations of their position may be
anxiously seeking how they can unify their interior
life and their program of external activity. This
unity of life cannot be brought about merely by an
outward arrangement of the works of the ministry
or by the practice of spiritual exercises alone, al-

---

17 Cf. 2 Cor. 1, 7.
18 Cf. 2 Cor. 1, 4.
19 Cf. 1 Cor. 10, 33.
20 Cf. John 3, 8.

though this may help to foster such unity. However, priests can achieve unity by following in the fulfillment of their ministry the example of Christ the Lord whose food was to do the will of him who sent him that he might perfect his work.[21]

The fact of the matter is that Christ is working through his ministers in order ceaselessly to do that same will of his Father in the world through the Church, and he therefore always remains the principle and source of the unity of their life. Hence, priests will achieve the unity of their life by joining themselves with Christ in the recognition of the Father's will and in the gift of themselves to the flock entrusted to them.[22] In this way, by adopting the role of the good shepherd, they will find in the practice of pastoral charity itself the bond of priestly perfection that will unify their life and activity. This pastoral charity[23] flows especially from the eucharistic sacrifice. This sacrifice is therefore the center and root of the whole life of the priest, so that the priestly soul strives to make its own what is enacted on the altar of sacrifice. But this cannot be achieved unless priests themselves penetrate ever more intimately through prayer into the mystery of Christ.

If priests are to make their unity of life a concrete reality, they should subject all their undertakings to the test of God's will[24]—that is, whether their projects are in conformity with the standards of the Church's Gospel mission. Faithfulness to Christ cannot be separated from faithfulness to his Church. Hence, pastoral charity demands that

---

21 Cf. John 4, 34.
22 Cf. 1 John 3, 16.
23 "Let it be the duty of love to shepherd the Lord's flock" (St. Augustine, *Tract. in Io.*, 123, 5: *P.L.* 35, 1967).
24 Cf. Rom. 12, 2.

priests, if they are not to run in vain,[25] should always work within the bond of union with the bishops and their other fellow priests. If they act in this manner, priests will find unity of life in the unity of the Church's own mission. In this way they will be united with their Lord and through him with the Father in the Holy Spirit, and can be filled with consolation and overflow with joy.[26]

II Special Spiritual Requirements in the Life of the Priest

Humility and Obedience

15. Among the virtues especially demanded by the ministry of priests must be reckoned that disposition of mind by which they are always prepared to seek not their own will but the will of him who has sent them.[27] The divine task, for the fulfillment of which they have been set apart by the Holy Spirit,[28] transcends all human strength and human wisdom, for "the foolish things of the world has God chosen to put to shame the 'wise'" (1 Cor. 1, 27).

Therefore, the true minister of Christ is conscious of his own weakness and labors in humility. He probes what is well pleasing to God[29] and, bound as it were in the Spirit,[30] he is guided in all things by the will of him who wishes all men to be saved. He is able to discover and carry out that will in the course of his daily routine by humbly placing himself at the service of all those who are

---

25 Cf. Gal. 2, 2.
26 Cf. 2 Cor. 7, 4.
27 Cf. John 4, 34; 5, 30; 6, 38.
28 Cf. Acts 13, 2.
29 Cf. Eph. 5, 10.
30 Cf. Acts 20, 22.

entrusted to his care by God in the office that has been committed to him and the variety of events that make up his life.

Since the priestly ministry is the ministry of the Church itself, it can only be fulfilled in the hierarchical union of the whole body of the Church. Therefore, pastoral charity urges priests to act within this communion and by obedience to dedicate their own will to the service of God and their fellow Christians. They will accept and carry out in the spirit of faith the commands and suggestions of the pope and of their bishop and other superiors. They will most gladly spend and be spent themselves[31] in whatever office is entrusted to them, even one humbler and poorer. By acting in this way they will preserve and strengthen the indispensable unity with their brothers in the ministry and especially with those whom the Lord has appointed to be the visible rulers of his Church. They will also work toward the building up of the body of Christ, which grows "through every joint of the system".[32] This obedience, which leads to the more mature freedom of the sons of God, by its nature demands that priests in the exercise of their duties should be moved by charity to prudently seek new methods of advancing the good of the Church. At the same time it also demands that, while putting forward their plans with confidence and being insistent to make known the needs of the flock entrusted to them, they should always be prepared to submit to the judgment of those who exercise the chief function in ruling God's Church.

By this humility and by responsible and willing obedience, priests conform themselves to Christ. They reproduce the sentiment of Jesus Christ who

32 Cf. Eph. 4, 11-16.

31 Cf. 2 Cor. 12, 15.

"emptied himself, taking the nature of a slave . . .
becoming obedient . . . even to death" (Phil. 2,
7–9) , and who by this obedience overcame and redeemed the disobedience of Adam, as the Apostle
declares: "For, just as by the disobedience of the
one man the many were constituted sinners, so also
by the obedience of the one the many will be constituted just" (Rom. 5, 19) .

Celibacy To Be Embraced and Esteemed as a Gift

16. Perfect and perpetual continence for the sake
of the kingdom of heaven was recommended by
Christ the Lord.[33] It has been freely accepted and
laudably observed by many Christians down through
the centuries as well as in our own time, and it
has always been highly esteemed in a special way
by the Church as a feature of priestly life. For it
is at once a sign of pastoral charity and an incentive
to it as well as being in a special way a source of
spiritual fruitfulness in the world.[34] It is true that
celibacy is not demanded of the priesthood by its
nature. This is clear from the practice of the primitive Church[35] and the tradition of the Eastern
Churches where, in addition to those—including all
bishops—who choose from the gift of grace to preserve celibacy, there are also many excellent married
priests. While recommending ecclesiastical celibacy,
this sacred Council does not by any means aim at
changing that contrary discipline which is lawfully
practiced in the Eastern Churches. Rather, the
Council affectionately exhorts all those who have
received the priesthood in the married state to per-

---

[33] Cf. Matt. 19, 12.

[34] Cf. *Dogmatic Constitution on the Church,* Nov. 21, 1964,
n. 42: *A.A.S.* 57 (1965), pp. 47-9.

[35] Cf. 1 Tim. 3, 2-5; Tit. 1, 6.

severe in their holy vocation and continue to devote their lives fully and generously to the flock entrusted to them.[36]

There are many ways in which celibacy is in harmony with the priesthood. The whole mission of the priest is dedicated to the service of the new humanity that Christ, the victor over death, raises up in the world through his Spirit and that has its origin "not of blood, nor of the will of the flesh, nor of the will of man, but of God" (John 1, 13). By preserving virginity or celibacy for the sake of the kingdom of heaven[37] priests are consecrated in a new and excellent way to Christ. They more readily cling to him with an undivided heart[38] and dedicate themselves more freely in him and through him to the service of God and of men. They are less encumbered in their service of his kingdom and of the task of heavenly regeneration. In this way they become better fitted for a broader acceptance of fatherhood in Christ.

By means of celibacy, then, priests profess before men their willingness to be dedicated with undivided loyalty to the task entrusted to them: namely, that of espousing the faithful to one husband and presenting them as a chaste virgin to Christ.[39] They recall that mystical marriage—established by God and destined to be fully revealed in the future—by which the Church holds Christ as her only Spouse.[40] Moreover, they are made a living sign of that world to come, already present

36 Cf. Pius XI, Encyclical Letter *Ad catholici sacerdotii*, Dec. 20, 1935: *A.A.S.* 28 (1936), p. 28.

37 Cf. Matt. 19, 12.

38 Cf. 1 Cor. 7, 32-34.

39 Cf. 2 Cor. 11, 2.

40 Cf. *Dogmatic Constitution on the Church*, Nov. 21, 1964, nn. 42, 44: *A.A.S.* 57 (1965), pp. 47-9, 50-1; *Decree on the Renewal of Religious Life*, Oct. 28, 1965, n. 12.

through faith and charity, a world in which the children of the resurrection shall neither be married nor take wives.[41]

For these reasons, based on the mystery of Christ and his mission, celibacy which at first was recommended to priests was afterward in the Latin Church imposed by law on all who were to be promoted to holy orders. This sacred Council approves and confirms this legislation insofar as those destined for the priesthood are concerned, trusting in the Spirit that the gift of celibacy, so appropriate to the priesthood of the New Testament, is liberally granted by the Father, provided that those who share Christ's priesthood through the sacrament of orders, and indeed the whole Church, ask for that gift humbly and earnestly.

This sacred Council also addresses an exhortation to all priests who, with trust in God's grace, have of their own free choice accepted consecrated celibacy after the example of Christ, that, holding fast to this state with courage and enthusiasm and faithfully persevering in it, they appreciate that glorious gift given them by the Father and so clearly extolled by the Lord,[42] and that they keep before their eyes the great mysteries signified and fulfilled in it. The more that perfect continence is considered by many people to be impossible in today's world, so much the more humbly and perseveringly, in union with the Church, should priests demand the grace of fidelity which is never denied to those who ask.

---

41 Cf. Luke 20, 35-36; Pius XI, Encyclical Letter *Ad catholici sacerdotii,* Dec. 20, 1935; *A.A.S.* 28 (1936), pp. 24-8; Pius XII, Encyclical Letter *Sacra virginitas,* Mar. 25, 1954: *A.A.S.* 46 (1954), pp. 169-72.

42 Cf. Matt. 19, 11.

At the same time priests should employ all the helps to fidelity, both supernatural and natural, that are available to everyone. They should especially never neglect to follow the rules of ascetical practice that are approved by the experience of the Church and are as necessary as ever in the modern world. Therefore, this sacred Council asks that not only priests but all the faithful cherish this precious gift of priestly celibacy, and that all of them beg of God always to lavish this gift abundantly on his Church.

Relations with the World and Worldy Goods:
Voluntary Poverty

17. By brotherly and friendly association with each other and with other people, priests can learn to cultivate human values and appreciate created goods as gifts of God. While living in the world they should still realize that, according to the Word of our Lord and Master, they are not of the world.[43] By using the world, then, as those who do not use it,[44] they will come to that liberty by which they will be freed from all inordinate anxiety and become docile to the divine voice in their daily life. From this liberty and docility grows that spiritual insight through which is found a right attitude to the world and to earthly goods.

This attitude is of great importance for priests, since the Church's mission is carried out in the midst of the world and created goods are absolutely necessary for man's personal progress. Let priests therefore be thankful for everything that the

---

43 Cf. John 17, 14-16.
44 Cf. 1 Cor. 7, 31.

heavenly Father has given them toward a proper standard of living. However, they ought to judge everything they meet in the light of faith so that they will be guided toward the right use of things in accordance with God's will and reject anything that is prejudicial to their mission.

As men whose "portion and inheritance" (Num. 18, 20) is the Lord, priests ought to use temporal goods only for those purposes to which the teaching of Christ and the direction of the Church allow them to be devoted.

Priests are to manage ecclesiastical property, properly so called, according to the nature of the case and the norm of ecclesiastical laws and with the help, as far as possible, of skilled laymen. They are to apply this property always to those purposes for the achievement of which the Church is allowed to own temporal goods. These purposes are the organization of divine worship, the provision of decent support for the clergy, and the exercise of works of the apostolate and of charity, especially for the benefit of those in need.[45]

Without prejudice to particular law,[46] priests as well as bishops are to use money, acquired by them on the occasion of their exercise of some ecclesiastical office, primarily for their own decent support and the fulfillment of the duties of their state. They should be willing to devote whatever is left over to the good of the Church or to works of charity. They are not to regard an ecclesiastical office as a source of profit and are not to spend the income accruing from it for increasing their own

---

[45] Council of Antioch, can. 25: *Mansi* 2, 1328; *Decree of Gratian,* c. 23, C. 12, q. 1 (ed. Friedberg I, pp. 684-5).

[46] This is to be understood especially of the laws and customs in force in the Eastern Churches.

private fortunes.[47] Therefore, priests, far from setting their heart on riches,[48] must always avoid all avarice and carefully refrain from all appearance of merchandising.

In fact, priests are invited to embrace voluntary poverty. By it they become more clearly conformed to Christ and more ready to devote themselves to their sacred ministry. For Christ, being rich, became poor for our sakes, that through his poverty we might be rich.[49] By their example the apostles gave testimony that the free gift of God was to be given freely.[50] They knew both how to abound and how to suffer want.[51] Even a certain common use of property, like the community of goods extolled in the history of the primitive Church,[52] provides an excellent opening for pastoral charity. By this way of life priests can laudably reduce to practice the spirit of poverty commended by Christ.

Guided then by the Spirit of the Lord, who anointed the Savior and sent him to preach the Gospel to the poor,[53] priests and bishops alike are to avoid everything that might in any way antagonize the poor. More than the rest of Christ's disciples, they are to put aside all appearance of vanity in their surroundings. They are to arrange their house in such a way that it never appears unapproachable to anyone and that no one, even the humblest, will ever be afraid to visit it.

---

[47] Council of Paris, a. 829, can. 15: M.G.H., Sect. III, *Concilia*, t. 2, p. 6, 622; Council of Trent, Sess. XXV, *De reform.*, ch. 1.

[48] Cf. Ps. 62, 11 (Vulgate 61).

[49] Cf. 2 Cor. 8, 9.

[50] Cf. Acts 8, 18-25.

[51] Cf. Phil. 4, 12.

[52] Cf. Acts 2, 42-47.

[53] Cf. Luke 4, 18.

III Means of Support for Priestly Life

Helps toward Fostering Interior Life

18. To enable them to foster union with Christ in all the circumstances of life, priests, in addition to the meaningful carrying out of their ministry, have at their disposal the means—both common and particular, new and old—which the Holy Spirit has never ceased to raise up among the People of God and which the Church recommends and in fact sometimes commands[54] for the sanctification of her members. Those actions by which Christians draw nourishment through the Word of God from the double table of holy Scripture and the eucharist hold a preeminent place above all spiritual aids.[55] Everyone knows how important their continuous use is for the personal sanctification of priests.

The ministers of sacramental grace are intimately united to Christ the Savior and pastor through the fruitful reception of the sacraments. This is especially true of the sacramental reception of penance. If it is prepared for by a daily examination of conscience, it is a powerful incentive to the essential conversion of heart to the love of the Father of mercies. Under the light of a faith nourished by spiritual reading, priests can diligently search for the signs of God's will and the inspirations of his grace in the varied events of life. In this way they will each day become more docile to the demands of the mission they have undertaken in the Holy Spirit. They can always find a wonderful example of such docility in the Blessed Virgin

---

[54] Cf. *C.I.C.,* canons 125ff.

[55] Cf. *Decree on the Renewal of Religious Life,* Oct. 28, 1965, n. 6; *Dogmatic Constitution on Divine Revelation,* Nov. 18, 1965, n. 21.

Mary who under the guidance of the Holy Spirit made a total dedication of herself for the mystery of the redemption of men.[56] Priests should always venerate and love her with a filial devotion and worship as the Mother of the Supreme and Eternal Priest, as Queen of Apostles and as protectress of their ministry.

As a help toward faithful fulfillment of their ministry, priests should love to talk daily with Christ the Lord in their visit to the most blessed sacrament and in their personal devotion to it. They should be glad to take time for spiritual retreats and have a high regard for spiritual direction. In various ways, particularly through the approved practice of mental prayer and the different forms of vocal prayer which they freely choose to practice, priests are to seek and perseveringly ask God for the true spirit of adoration. By this spirit they themselves and with them the people entrusted to their care will unite themselves with Christ, the mediator of the New Testament, and be able as adopted sons to cry "Abba, Father" (Rom. 8, 15).

Study and Pastoral Knowledge

19. Priests are warned by the bishop in the ceremony of ordination that they are to be "mature in knowledge" and that their teaching should be "a spiritual medicine for the People of God".[57] Since a sacred minister's knowledge should be sacred in the sense of being derived from a sacred source and directed to a sacred purpose, such knowledge

---

[56] Cf. *Dogmatic Constitution on the Church,* Nov. 21, 1964, n. 65: *A.A.S.* 57 (1965) , pp. 64-5.

[57] Cf. "Ordination of a Priest" in the *Roman Pontifical.*

is therefore primarily drawn from the reading and meditation of Sacred Scripture.[58] It is also fruitfully nourished by the study of the Fathers and Doctors of the Church and the other ancient records of tradition. Moreover, if priests are to give adequate answers to the problems discussed by people at the present time, they should be well versed in the statements of the Church's magisterium and especially those of the councils and the popes. They should also consult the best of the approved writers on the science of theology.

Secular culture and even sacred science are advancing at an unprecedented rate in our time. Priests are therefore urged to the adequate and continuous perfection of their knowledge of things divine and human. In this way they will prepare themselves to enter with greater advantage into dialogue with their contemporaries.

To facilitate study and the more effective learning of methods of evangelization and the apostolate, every care should be taken to provide priests with suitable aids. Examples of these are the organization of courses or congresses according to the conditions of each territory, the establishment of centers designed for pastoral studies, the founding of libraries and the proper direction of studies by suitable persons.

In addition, bishops, either individually or in collaboration with others, should consider more effective ways of arranging for their priests to be able to attend a course of study at certain times, especially for a few years after ordination.[59] The

---

[58] Cf. *Dogmatic Constitution on Divine Revelation,* Nov. 18, 1965, n. 25.

[59] This course is not the same as the pastoral course to be completed immediately after ordination which is discussed in the *Decree on Priestly Training,* Oct. 28, 1965, n. 22.

aim of the course would be to give them an opportunity of increasing their knowledge of pastoral methods and theological science, and at the same time of strengthening their spiritual life and sharing their pastoral experiences with their brother priests.[60] By these and other suitable aids special attention may also be given to helping newly appointed parish priests, as well as priests assigned to new pastoral work or sent to another diocese or country.

Finally, bishops should be careful to see that some priests devote themselves to a deeper study of the sacred sciences. This will ensure that there will never be any lack of suitable teachers for the education of clerics. It will also ensure that the rest of the priests and the faithful will be helped in acquiring the knowledge of religion necessary for them and that the sound progress in sacred studies so very necessary for the Church will be encouraged.

The Provision of Just Remuneration for Priests

20. Completely devoted as they are to the service of God in the fulfillment of the office entrusted to them, priests are entitled to receive a just remuneration, for "the laborer deserves his wages" (Luke 10, 7),[61] and "the Lord directed that those who preach the Gospel should have their living from the Gospel" (1 Cor. 9, 14). For this reason, insofar as provision is not made from some other source for the just remuneration of priests, the

---

60 Cf. *Decree on the Pastoral Office of Bishops in the Church,* Oct. 28, 1965, n. 16.

61 Cf. Matt. 10, 10; 1 Cor. 9, 7; 1 Tim. 5, 18.

faithful are bound by a real obligation of seeing to it that the necessary provision for a decent and fitting livelihood for the priests is available. This obligation arises from the fact that it is for the benefit of the faithful that the priests are working. Bishops are bound to warn the faithful of their obligation in this connection. They should also see to it—either individually for their own dioceses, or, better still, by several acting together for a common territory—that rules are drawn up by which due provision is made for the decent support of those who hold or have held any office in the service of God.

Taking into consideration the conditions of different places and times as well as the nature of the office they hold, the remuneration to be received by each of the priests should be fundamentally the same for all living in the same circumstances. It should be in keeping with their status and in addition should give priests the means not only of providing properly for the salary of those who devote themselves to their service but also of personally assisting in some way those who are in need. From its very beginnings the Church has always held this ministry to the poor in great honor. Moreover, priests' remuneration should be such as to allow the priest a proper vacation each year. The bishop should see to it that priests are able to have this vacation.

However, the greatest importance should be given to the office that sacred ministers fulfill. For this reason the so-called system of benefices is to be abandoned or else reformed in such a way that the beneficiary aspect—that is, the right to the revenues attached to the endowment of the office—shall be regarded as secondary and the principal emphasis in law given to the ecclesiastical office itself. In the future this should be understood as any office conferred in a permanent fashion and to be exercised for a spiritual purpose.

Common Funds To Be Set Up: Social Security for Priests To Be Organized

21. The example of the faithful in the primitive Church of Jerusalem should be always kept in mind. There "they had all things in common" (Acts 4, 32), and "distribution was made to each, according as anyone had need" (Acts 4, 35). It is therefore an excellent arrangement—at least in places where the support of the clergy depends completely or to a great extent on the offerings of the faithful—that the money offered in this way should be collected by some kind of diocesan agency. The bishop would administer this agency with the help of priests appointed for this purpose, aided also by lay experts in economics where the advantage of such appointment may make it advisable.

It is also desirable that as far as possible there should be set up in each diocese or region a common fund to enable bishops to satisfy obligations to people employed in the service of the Church and to meet the various needs of the diocese. Also, from this fund richer dioceses would be able to help poorer ones so that the abundance of the one would supply the want of the other.[62] This common fund should be made up mainly of money from the offerings of the faithful as well as from those coming from other sources to be determined by law.

---

[62] Cf. 2 Cor. 8, 14.

Moreover, in countries where social security has not yet been adequately organized for the benefit of clergy, episcopal conferences are to make provision, in harmony with ecclesiastical and civil law, for the setting up of diocesan organizations (even federated with one another), or organizations for different dioceses grouped together, or an association catering for the whole territory: the purpose of these being that, under the supervision of the hierarchy, satisfactory provision be made both for suitable insurance and what is called "health assistance" and for the proper support of priests who suffer from sickness, ill health or old age.

Priests should assist this organization when it has been established, moved by a spirit of solidarity with their brother priests, sharing their hardships,[63] and at the same time realizing that in this way they can, without any anxiety for their future, practice poverty with a readier appreciation of the Gospel and devote themselves completely to the salvation of souls. Those responsible should do their utmost to have such organizations combined on an international scale, so as to give them more stability and strength and promote their wider diffusion.

CONCLUSION

22. This sacred Council, while keeping in mind the joys of the priestly life, cannot pass over the difficulties that priests also encounter in the circumstances of their life today. It also knows how much economic and social conditions and even

---

63 Cf. Phil. 4, 14.

men's morals are being transformed and how much men's sense of values is undergoing change. Hence it is that the Church's ministers, and even sometimes the faithful, in the midst of this world feel themselves estranged from it and are anxiously seeking suitable methods and words by which they may be able to communicate with it. The new obstacles opposing the faith, the apparent fruitlessness of the work done, the bitter loneliness they experience—these can bring for priests the danger of a feeling of frustration.

However, this world as it is, entrusted today to the Church as the object of its love and service —this is the world God has so loved as to give his only-begotten Son for it.[1] The truth is that this world, caught as it is in the grip of much sin and yet also enriched with many possibilities, provides the Church with the living stones[2] that are built together into a habitation of God in the Spirit.[3] While urging the Church to open new avenues of approach to the modern world, the same Holy Spirit also suggests and fosters suitable adaptations of the priestly ministry.

Let priests remember that in carrying out their task they are never alone but are supported by the almighty power of God. Believing in Christ who has called them to share in his priesthood, let them devote themselves to their office with complete trust, knowing that God has the power to increase charity in them.[4] Let them remember, too, that they have their brothers in the priesthood

---

[1] Cf. John 3, 16.

[2] Cf. 1 Pet. 2, 5.

[3] Cf. Eph. 2, 22.

[4] Cf. "Ordination of a Priest" in the *Roman Pontifical.*

and indeed the faithful of the entire world as allies.

All priests cooperate in carrying out God's saving plan, the mystery of Christ or the sacrament hidden from eternity in God.[5] Only gradually is this mystery carried into effect by the united efforts of the different ministries for the building up of the body of Christ until the measure of its age be fulfilled. Since all these truths are hidden with Christ in God,[6] it is especially by faith that they can be perceived, for the leaders of the People of God must walk by faith, following the example of the faithful Abraham who by faith "obeyed by going out into a place which he was to receive for an inheritance; and he went out, not knowing where he was going" (Heb. 11, 8).

Indeed, the dispenser of the mysteries of God can be compared to the man who cast the seed into the earth, of whom the Lord said that he should "sleep and rise, night and day, and the seed should sprout and grow without his knowing it" (Mark 4, 27). The Lord Jesus who said: "Take courage; I have overcome the world" (John 16, 33), did not by these words promise complete victory to his Church in this world. This sacred Council rejoices that the earth which has been sown with the seed of the Gospel is now bringing forth fruit in many places under the guidance of the Spirit of the Lord. This Spirit is filling the world and has stirred up a truly missionary spirit in the hearts of many priests and faithful. For all this the sacred Council affectionately offers its thanks to all the priests of the world: "Now to him who is able to accomplish all things in a

5 Cf. Eph. 3, 9.
6 Cf. Col. 3, 3.

measure far beyond what we ask or conceive, in keeping with the power that is at work in us— to him be glory in the Church and in Christ Jesus" (Eph. 3, 20-21).

* * *

Each and every point stated in this Decree has satisfied the fathers of the sacred Council. And we, by the authority bestowed on us by Christ, together with the venerable fathers, approve it in the Holy Spirit, we decree it and we enact it; and we order the promulgation, to God's glory, of what has been enacted synodically.

Rome, in St. Peter's Basilica, December 7, 1965
Paul, Bishop of the Catholic Church

(The fathers' signatures follow)

Study-Club Questions

1. What is the threefold priestly character of the entire body of Christ?
2. What is the purpose of the priesthood of orders?
3. How is the ministerial priesthood primarily and fully realized in the bishop?
4. How can priests live on earth with other men as brothers?
5. What are the three major functions of an ordained priest?
6. Is there any inherent tension in the bishop-priest relationship?
7. The obedience of a priest must be the active virtue of a mature man. Explain.
8. Briefly discuss the theological basis of the unity that should exist among priests.
9. What is the difference between the diocesan clergy and the regular clergy?
10. Mention some possible areas of friction between older and younger priests.
11. Why is it necessary to have some sort of community life among the clergy?
12. What is the fundamental bond of unity between the clergy and the laity?
13. How can the principle of collegiality, affirmed in the *Constitution on the Church,* be applied at every level of the Church's life?

156

14. Why should John Wesley's dictum, "The world is my parish," express the attitude of every Catholic priest?

15. Whose obligation is it to encourage and develop vocations to the priestly ministry?

16. Briefly discuss three specific recommendations for priestly holiness contained in Chapter III.

17. Why should the demands of the pastoral ministry provide the primary motivation for priestly asceticism?

18. What is the norm for judging the value of one's pastoral activities?

19. Is passive receptivity a Christian virtue?

20. Why is the virtue of celibacy especially suitable for the priesthood?

21. Mention some possible ways in which priests can channel their love into new and creative ways of serving and loving the community.

22. How does the Council invite priests to embrace voluntary poverty?

23. Briefly discuss the Council's observations on the continuing intellectual formation of priests.

24. How do the letter and the spirit of this Decree suggest a radical rethinking of our present system of clerical remuneration?

25. In the light of what other conciliar documents must this Decree be studied?